The Strategic Casino Host

Jackie Parker, MBA

Happy to **H**elp
Organized
Strategic
Thoughtful

Also by the Author:

Casino Host Goals: A Strategic approach to Player Development

How to Become a Casino Host

ISBN-9781987794519

Dedication

With much love to **Jill Parker**
for inspiration, encouragement,
and teaching me to laugh.

Acknowledgements

A special call-out to Amy Hudson.

A big thank you to those who
generously contributed to this book:

Allyson Howey
Colleen Cutler
Curtis Patnode
Jim Sulima
Joseph De Vito III
Lorena Castaneda
Matthew Clark Oxford
Susan Kesel
Travis Hankins

Thank you Kayle McKenzie for your suggestions
about Organizing Events.

Thank you Jatonia Ziegler for permission
to publish your article on 5 Tips for Dinner Parties.

And a thank you to everyone that
uses our **PowerHost CRM** software
and gives suggestions on how to
empower Hosts.

Table of Contents

Chapter 1. INTRODUCTION

"The future belongs to those who learn more skills and combine them in creative ways." Robert Greene

Congratulations for taking the time to read this book and invest in your personal growth!

Successful people invest time and money to explore ideas, learn new skills, and change their perception on how they see themselves, their role, and their career. You don't have to agree with everything in this book; but you should think about what is said and then decide on your own beliefs and approach.

This book is written for **new** Casino Hosts to explore the depth and breadth of your role, and for **experienced** Casino Hosts to take your game to the next level and prepare for the future. If you are a manager, this book may express ideas that you take for granted, and that you can use in coaching your team.

I encourage you to take a pen and draw circles all over this book wherever you recognize an area for personal improvement because this is a manual for personal growth. You will find a self-assessment tool at the end of each Chapter.

The book is organized around these four themes:

H – Happy to Help

O – Organized

S – Strategic

T – Thoughtful

In **Happy to Help**, we explore what it means to **Help** the guest while meeting the financial demands of the Casino.

And we explore the need to be **Happy** to Help because you will burn out if you don't have a genuine passion for the role.

In **Organized,** we talk about techniques to manage your day because the role of being a Host is so detail oriented and demanding. You are constantly dragged into tactical tasks such as resolving customer service issues, approving Hotel comps, making reservations, and running events. You have to complete all of these daily tasks and also carve out the time to be strategic so that you can meet and exceed your goals.

In **Strategic**, we describe how the organized Host will take pro-active steps to meet their Goals, also referred to as KPI's. A key performance indicator, KPI, is a way that Management measures your results, from booking room nights to increasing trips. The Strategic Host will consistently meet and exceed their KPIs to position themselves for promotions and new opportunities.

In **Thoughtful**, we talk both about how to be thoughtful with your guests, which means using your Emotional Intelligence, but also being thoughtful about your role and how to stay out of trouble.

In the Final Chapter, we discuss how to plan for your next career move. You might want to stay as a Host, move into Management, or build out your personal guest list and brand yourself as a Player Development Executive.

This book is full of practical advice from Hosts, Managers, Player Development Executives, and VP's Player Development. They gave their ideas and time generously because they have a passion for this profession!

Why not join them in the Casino Player Development Association (C-PDA) so we can grow this profession together? Contact me at jparker@harvesttrends.com

Chapter 2. OVERVIEW

Let's be honest! It requires a wide range of skills to be a strategic and successful Casino Host!

You have to sell; yourself, the amenities, the hotel rooms, and the events.

You have to stay upbeat and energetic in your tone and attitude despite brutal shifts and a lack of budget.

You need empathy to understand total strangers.

You need a phenomenal memory for faces, names, and all the little details that maintain a relationship with each guest; including their preferences, their occupation, and the names of their loved ones.

You have to be a good communicator, both verbal and written.

You may think of yourself as a People Person, but a Strategic Host also has to be a Numbers Person.

You have to quickly weigh circumstances and crunch numbers to make decisions, the results of which your players will take personally.

You have to be ever mindful of the policies, procedures, regulatory concerns, ethical considerations and other guidelines by which you have to conduct your business.

You have to think like an entrepreneur and develop your book of business, while abiding with your casino's rules for reinvestment.

You have to develop solid working relationships with people around the casino to help you meet your guests' needs. You won't be able to pull weight in the steakhouse if you have fallen out with the Director of Food and Beverage.

"Being resourceful means knowing the ins and outs of your own property...who you need to talk to in order to get things done and where to go to get what you need for your players.

> Sometimes it's a cocktail server who you need to ask for a favor for your player or a housekeeping attendant who you want to do something special in a hotel room. In order to get these, you need to be courteous and thankful to all fellow associates because you never know when you might need a small favor from them that will make a big difference to your player."

You have to be very confident and wear a thick skin because players will try to roll over you to get Comps and freebies, and their approach will include getting very upset with you.

> "You have to be compassionate but tough. Not giving someone what they want while ensuring they are still happy is an art. It's easy to say yes but not so easy not to give them what they have asked for while keeping them happy and wanting to stay a guest of your company."

And this list of necessary skills will only grow longer as we work our way through this book!

But, to keep it simple, you are perfecting all of these different skills to achieve just one ultimate goal! Which is to use your personal relationship with each guest to create loyalty.

Your #1 responsibility?
*Develop **loyalty** in your guests.*

Here it is in a nutshell; create personal relationships so your guests are your fans. And your fans won't want to disappoint you by going to your competition; in fact, they will even feel guilty in case you find out!

> "One of the most legendary hosts I ever heard of was a gentleman who had left my first property before I was hired. He was legendary because he remembered things about his players that most people wouldn't.
>
> The story that I was told first about him has stuck with me for many years: he had a guest whose dog, Jake, had

suffered a broken leg which had to be put in a cast for several weeks.

This host sent the guest a handwritten card to wish Jake a speedy recovery and to express his dismay over Jake's injury.

Rumor has it that the patron refused to go to another casino as long as this gentleman was his host because he'd taken the time to send well wishes to the guest's dog, who was the man's four-legged child in a sense."

As we go through this book and explore all of the different aspects of your role, recall this story and think about how to develop such an intense feeling of **loyalty** in your guests. The good news is that all it took was for the Host to pay attention and then take a simple action.

The Power of Personal Loyalty

Why do General Managers invest in hiring a Player Development team? To create customer loyalty. Why is it so important to build personal loyalty to a Host? Because of ever increasing competition.

"Host skills are based on relationships. Built to gain a player's trust and want to come and spend their gaming wallet. The skill of a player development executive is to tailor and package the best offers overall to make a player choose your property over the competition. This is what sales is all about - to increase revenue per guest."

The Cinema of my youth had lines around the block and could cram the audience into small seats, narrow rows, and a large auditorium showing just one movie-title per week. 'Going to the Movies' was THE exciting outing, and the Cinema did not have to compete with other forms of entertainment. But you know this has all changed for the Cinema.

What is going to change for the Casino?

We have so much choice of entertainment including on-line gaming from the comfort of our own home. So why go out at all, and why pick a casino? Why pick your casino? Because of loyalty to you!

As more and more casinos open across America, the most important thing to provide to VIP players is a superior customer service experience. High net worth gamblers can buy almost anything they want, but no-one can buy an experience and, to quote the Beatles, 'Money Can't Buy Me Love'.

- ✓ A host can make more inviting for a player to return to a particular property than any other service the casino can offer.

- ✓ A host can find out whether a particular guest enjoys tournaments and be sure to invite them.

- ✓ A host can let them know when it looks like their favorite progressive has reached that 'sweet' amount.

- ✓ A host can know that the guest likes lobster and give them a call when there is a special offer coming up.

- ✓ A host can get an unhappy guest to share the tale of their bad experience and convince them to give your property another chance to get it right.

The Direct Mail team can send out the offers but only a host can use a well-constructed phone call to provide the final push and get the patron to commit to the trip.

There is nothing as effective as a casino host when it comes to bringing back players with high worth. And if the relationship is strong enough, then the player will even feel a tinge of guilt if they play somewhere else! And, of course, your best players are also the best players for your local competition. **You are competing with the PD team at those other casinos!**

These players expect much more than coupons and promotions as a 'reward' for their patronage. They know they are worth a lot to you and expect to be treated as such.

This requires you to be thoughtful about each guest and consider how to make them feel important:

> "If I know a guest is coming in at 9pm, then I am out at Valet Parking at 8:45pm, to be ready to greet them with a smile. I don't have to spend the evening with them but I do have to be there to welcome them."

This is a great example, from a Player Development Executive, of how creating a great experience does not have to include an offer but does require **your personal time and attention.**

Each day, as you approach the challenge of creating personal relationships, focus on creating a warm and positive experience for your guests, and focus less on what you can 'give' them.

> "A good Host is able to anticipate guests' needs: Planning ahead and walking through the guests' trip prior to their arrival and anticipating possible pit falls and/or finding areas in which to enhance their experience."

The Casino has a limit on what you can give in comps, events, tickets, amenities. But there is no limit on the care and consideration that you can give the guest in the way you greet them, treat them, and follow up with them.

"I've learned that people will forget what you said, people will forget what you did, but people will never forget how you made them feel."
Maya Angelou

Self-Assessment

Before you read on, grab a pen and complete this self-assessment. Where are your areas for improvement?

Skill	Always	Most of the time	Rarely
I stay upbeat and energetic in my tone and attitude			
I have the empathy to understand total strangers.			
I am a good communicator, both verbal and written.			
I can remember faces, names, and details.			
I can quickly crunch numbers to make decisions.			
I have studied the policies, procedures, and regulations.			
I have excellent working relationships with other departments.			
I think like an entrepreneur.			
I focus on creating long-term loyalty with guests via personal relationship.			
I create an experience that money cannot buy.			

Chapter 3. H IS FOR HAPPY TO HELP

"When you find what you love, and you find people that will support you, you're living the dream, whatever you do" Cole Swindell

If it is in your nature to be happy to help, then you are in the right profession! You can excel in player development if the demands of the job are aligned with your underlying personality and goals.

> "First and foremost, you must be outgoing and enjoy people in general. I don't believe that is something you can fake. "

You will have some players who visit regularly, even daily, because they are filling a void in their lives. They come to the Property, perhaps by limo because they can't get around, and they are happy to lose money in return for being welcomed into the family. As their Casino Host, you can bring some warmth into their lives. Does that seem important to you? Does that seem genuine to you?

> "You have to be is passionate about what you do. You have to truly enjoy the industry, the job, and what you do in order to be successful. You have to be able to draw excitement from accommodating others and ensuring they are excited and having fun.
>
> This will not only make your job easier, but you will be a better host as your relationships will be natural and true."

In an interview for this book, a manager was describing the qualities that he looks for in a Casino Host and then he finished with this great line:

> "Don't tell me what you want to be.
> Tell me what you want to **do**"

What do you want to do? Do you want to make a difference in some people's lives, do you want to be part of successful team that grows the business, do you want to learn and explore your own creativity?

> "It is a profession where you can make decent money. Don't do it for the money. Do it because you enjoy people and **you want to ensure they have the best experience possible** while ensuring they are profitable for the company."

What do we mean by an experience?

The Casino provides an escape from everyday life with sounds and lighting to stimulate and arouse our senses. The decor is designed to be upmarket and to make people feel that they are in a 'special' place. In addition to experiencing the glamour, people want to feel important. So many people feel worn-down, under-appreciated, and that they are slipping behind compared to the stars of the Reality TV shows. When they walk into the Casino, they can feel important again and especially if they are greeted warmly.

> "Our secret weapon is our security guards. They are the first employees that a guest meets as they walk in the door, and we train the guards to welcome each and every guest with a big smile."

As the Casino Host, you want the valuable player to think of you as part of this special world. They are deliberately taking time away from their job, family, relationships, stresses and strains, to give you their entertainment dollars. They want their Casino Host to consistently give them an unconditional and reassuring warm welcome. And to develop their loyalty, you must become an important part of their escape.

Look the guest in the eye and make them feel as if they are the only person in the room. Hold her gaze and keep asking questions about her favorite subject which is herself. When it's your turn to reply, repeat what you've just learned in your own words:

> *"Beth, I can see why you feel so frustrated about the delay in remodeling your home. I am glad you came here tonight to relax. I hope you have a great time"*

The truly great Host will remember this conversation, for weeks and months!, and ask Beth about the home renovation when he sees her next.

Make a Connection, Not an Offer

> "Don't come out of the gate with an offer. You don't want to be seen as a walking ATM, spitting out gifts, so don't behave like one. When you approach those players on the gaming floor, or when you reach an inactive player by phone, don't automatically offer free play or a buffet comp. Player development is about relationships, and it isn't your job to be Santa Claus."

Talk with the guest. Learn why he visits your property instead of a competitor's. Find out why he doesn't like the buffet or never brings his wife with him. Make a connection instead of an offer.

A generic definition of a Host is "a person who receives or entertains other people as guests." As a Casino Host, you are receiving and entertaining other people as guests at your Resort Casino.

Are you a friend? Of course not. But you do have to be human being and share a little of yourself.

> "Be personal (about yourself): This one is tricky and comes with caution but when I first started I always only asked about the players...what was new, how they were doing, etc. Over time, I realized I knew a lot of personal things about them, but they didn't know anything personal about me. And it wasn't because they didn't want to know, I think they thought they would be prying.
>
> After developing these relationships, I found it was okay, actually welcomed by the guests, to talk about myself. Sometimes they only see you as an 'employee', but they eventually see you as a 'person'.

> Relationships and friendships are about reciprocity—if the conversations are only one way then you won't break beyond the customer/employee statuses.
>
> This is most easily accomplished by taking them off the casino floor to a dinner or event. Many of the conversations on the casino floor are transactional. I've learned more about players in the first 5 minutes of a personal dinner than I have in 5 months on the casino floor."

For those of you that are new to the role of Casino Host, be careful to always set boundaries around your interactions with guests.

Don't get too friendly or you can easily cross a line that leads to no end of trouble with your reputation, your job, the Gaming Regulator, and even with law enforcement.

Don't make them feel too important or they will feel entitled to throw their weight around and be demanding.

Don't blow hot and cold or they might feel rejected and want to complain about you.

Your outreach via phone, text, and email should also include regular and consistent efforts to maintain a connection. Don't just reach out when you have an offer and you want their participation. So, make a note to call Beth in a few days and ask her about that re-modeling project. Investing just three minutes of your time on the phone with Beth will definitely help to develop her loyalty.

Focus on Being Helpful, not on Helping

You should always focus on making the guest _feel_ helped and not on delivering whatever it is that they want. Why? Because you might not be able to deliver on what they want. But if you can deliver, then you win double brownie points!

Avoid this trap, raised by an Executive Host:

> "The main reason I see hosts fail is because they oversell their capabilities and underperform or otherwise forget the task. It's great to come across as a 'Johnny on the spot' individual who swiftly takes care of any and all needs, but make sure you can finish what you start. Don't lead off every answer with, 'of course', or 'you got it!'. Give yourself some wiggle room with an open-ended answer like, 'let me see what I can do for you'. This allows you to work with your casino team in case there are issues that would otherwise prevent you from handling the request."

Yes, you will get a nice big smile from the guest if you say, "You got it!" in response to their request for an upgrade. But then you may have the hard task of going back and saying, "I cannot do this".

If you cannot deliver on your promise, then you need to own that outcome. Do not wimp out and give one of two excuses. If you say "My boss would not let me" then you make yourself look powerless. And if you say "The casino doesn't allow that' then you look ignorant because you should have known that to start with. Either way, you have not established yourself as a helpful, influential, Casino Host.

The Executive Host that we quote above, is recommending that you always say, "Let me see what I can do for you". If you can deliver the upgrade, then great. If not, you return to the guest and emphasize that you did what you said you would do. You did try, and you will always try.

In summary, focus on how you make them feel and not on what you can actually give them. Using this approach, you leave the guest feeling that you tried, and you will try again for them in the future.

Make a No Sound like a Yes

Practice how to refuse without actually saying no. For example, if a customer asks you for a comp to a hotel suite and they don't meet the criteria, you don't say No. You say something like "What I can offer you at this time, based on your play, is X, Y, Z".

It's important not to shut them down but use their request as an introduction to tell them how much they'll have to play in order to earn the thing they want. Treat it as a learning moment!

For example, "Based on your play, I can offer you a buffet. As soon as you reach the Silver level, I can offer you that 2 for 1 meal. Do you know how close you are to Silver and how to get there?"

This feels like you are trying to help, because you are identifying what you can do, and you are offering to help them to understand what they have to do, to get what they want. They might not like the outcome, but they need to see and believe that it is fair.

 Always educate the guest on what they need to do in order to get what they want.

Put the ball back in the player's court, so to speak, and then the 'no' doesn't have to be said. Empower the guest to earn what's necessary to have their wish fulfilled.

> "Be very careful with how you say No. You don't want to hurt someone's feelings and not be aware of that, because they will simply play more at a different property and you won't notice unless you are paying strong attention to trips and ADT. If you do realize, and if you can get them to tell you what happened, you are going to have to work twice as hard to win them back. You also need to be aware of how to deal with different cultures because some people cannot afford to lose face."

Don't try to explain what theoretical means, or how comps and offers are calculated. You will get yourself into the weeds, and potentially into a debate with a cantankerous player about what makes sense and how the competition does it. Instead, focus on explaining what the guest has to do, to get what they want, at your Casino.

This means that you need to memorize the different levels of the Player Club, the necessary number of points to achieve each level, and the detailed benefits at each level. If you have this information at your fingertips, then you will speak with confidence.

Track the Direct Mail Program

In addition to knowing the Club Benefits inside and out, you can benefit from understanding the strategies of your direct mail program.

> What is the Direct Mail program?
>
> Each month, the Casino looks at the number of trips, and amount of Theo, from each player over the last 3, 6, 12 months or whatever. The players are put into groups, called Segments, and they are sent offers for free play, for free or discounted food, for free or discounted hotel rooms etc.

Your players care very much about their offers and whether they seem to be 'fair' and how they compare to your competition. They are going to be griping to you about their treatment and you need to be prepared with your responses.

You don't need to know all the nitty gritty details, but you do need to understand the overall logic behind the calculations.

You need to find out, at the highest level, whether the Direct Mail program is based on ADT, ATT, Total Theo, or a combination of ADT, Theo, Actual, and Trips.

> What is Average Trip Theo (ATT)?
>
> Imagine that Jose plays on Friday, Saturday, Sunday with a total theo of 3000. If the system tracks Days, then Jose has played 3 days. His ADT = 3000 / 3 = 1000. But if the system tracks Trips then Jose has made 1 weekend trip. His ATT = 3000/1 = 3000.
>
> Sophisticated player tracking systems can be configured so if Manuel lives locally, we think of Saturday, Sunday, Monday as 3 trips. ATT = 1000. But Jose lives 4 hours away, so we assume he had to stay over, and Saturday, Sunday, Monday are 1 trip.

Let's discuss two scenarios in which the logic behind the Direct Mail program can impact your guests. In our imaginary world, the Sandy Palace Casino has a simplistic approach and bases offers on ADT (average daily theo) over the last 3 months. The Direct Mail team add up all of Colleen, Robin and Bill's Total Theo over the last 3 months and divides it by the number of days that they played.

1. Colleen plays every Friday night because that is how she relaxes at the end of her stressful week. She has a budget in mind and plays consistently each week for 12 weeks.

    Each Friday, her Theo is around 300 so her ADT = 300. The Direct Mail team will send her an offer based on the hope they can incent her to add an additional trip at 300+. In reality, she takes that free play and uses it next Friday. She won't ever add a trip.

    As a Host, you are unlikely to hear from Colleen about her offers because they are consistent.

2. Robin plays on Fridays and Saturdays with her best friends. She also has a budget in mind and her Theo varies from 300 to 350, so her ADT would be 325, similar to Colleen.

    However, Robin decides to take her free play offers and her F&B coupons and make an extra trip on Monday and Wednesday evenings on her way home from work. She eats for free, doesn't play for long because she has to get home and maybe puts an additional $25 into the slots after she has burned through her free play.

    Robin is now penalized by her behavior because she has dragged down her ADT from 325 to (300+350+25+25) / 4 = 175. In January, she just plays weekends and receives February offers for 300+ ADT. In February, she adds her small trips on Monday and Wednesdays, and her March offers drop because they are based on 175+ ADT.

    As a Host, you will hear complaints from Robin because her offers will vary based on her behavior from month to month.

As an ethical Host, keeping the casino's business objectives in mind, should you really coach Robin on how to play to beat the 'system'?

3. In this final scenario, Bill is unhappy with the competition and he comes over to try the Sandy Palace. You are assigned to groom Bill because he is a 300+ player. Bill plays for a few weekends and he is pretty happy with his offers based on 300+ ADT.

    You keep working on building a relationship with Bill and he decides to move his play from the competition to the Sandy Palace. Overall, Bill now brings a lot more total Theo. But, unfortunately, like Robin, this means he is also bringing some smaller trips to your Property and suddenly his offers drop in value and he is mad and threatens to go back to the competition. Especially as the competition now considers Bill to be a 'fader' and they will bump their offers up to lure him back.

If you are new to this arena, then talk to your peers and Manager and do some research about what is happening at your property and with your competition. Just as gas stations and supermarkets compete with each other by having 'specials' so do casinos compete with each other by fluctuating their offers.

If you are an experienced host, then you have seen all of these scenarios and more.

"Parameters should be set to not punish a guest. Casino marketing periodically clash when overlapping promotional offers and redemption days. Of course, the idea is to drive more trips but while it manipulates a guest's trip habits, it won't necessarily change their budget allowance. For example, the marketing department creates a gift giveaway promo on Tuesday, hot seat drawing Wednesday, following big cash giveaway promo on Saturday. A guest who typically frequents your casino once a week (weekend) may want that free gift and show up to redeem it but not have time to play. This guest may show up the last couple hours after work to attend a hot seat drawing, only able to play

20% of their usual playtime. Now this guest shows up their usual time on the weekend for the big promotion and can play to their FULL extent. Breaking it down, this guest's total theoretical may raise incrementally, but ADT will most likely drop. Was this the guest's fault? Not necessarily, as they are just doing what the marketing dept wants. Is it the Host's fault? Definitely not, as they do not create the promotional schedule."

At the end of the day, you must support the intention of your Direct Mail program and not undermine their approach by coaching your guests. That said, you can talk to your manager about what you see as the adverse side effects of the program and empower them to speak to the Marketing manager with detailed examples.

It is not easy to craft a direct marketing strategy that meets the goal of driving more trips without having bad side effects on some guests. Have you heard of the *Law of Unintended Consequences*? The Direct Mail team intended to make Robin happy and to drive additional trips. Well, they did drive additional trips, of low value, and Robin is very unhappy. Your role is to share what you hear about specific players, so the strategy can be improved but do not present your feedback in a negative way. The relationship between Direct Marketing and Player Development needs to be a constructive give and take.

Changing Criteria

Over time, your players will realize what they can expect based on their play and they will develop an expectation that they are owed these offers. They see the offers as the Thank You owed to them for their previous play whereas the Casino sees the offers as an investment in future play. (You will hear management refer to this as the Entitlement Mindset. Valuable players can develop the belief that they are entitled to great offers.)

Unfortunately for you, the Direct Mail team will occasionally change the criteria and the amounts, and then your players will feel cheated because they played just as much as usual.

You don't want to be blind-sided and you need to be ready with an answer that will focus on what they player has to do, to get what they want. Unlike the Point Levels, the segments and criteria are not public knowledge, so you definitely cannot get into a detailed description and can only suggest a general recommendation to 'play more'. This lack of transparency makes the conversation particularly hard.

Be proactive and help your manager to create a collaborative relationship with the Direct Mail team so that you are not blind-sided. In some Casinos, the PD team even gets to review the offers, and make adjustments for coded players, before the mailer is sent out. This is very cumbersome for the Direct Mail team, so they won't be keen to do this.

The Value of a Player

If you want a lively discussion in your next team meeting, then initiate this debate about who is most profitable?

Dee who plays 20 days each month with a 100 ADT and receives a free buffet?

Or, Kenny who plays twice a month with a 1000 ADT but demands the penthouse and a dinner comp, and drinks all the Jack Daniels in the VIP room?

Their total Theo per month is the same, 2000, but Dee's expenses are less, so she is more profitable to the Casino. In most Properties, Kenny will have a VIP Host because of his 500 ADT and Dee will not, with her 100 ADT. Perhaps this makes sense because Dee is fairly 'saturated', she is already playing 20 days per month, so a Host could not drive many more 100+ trips. Whereas there is definitely an opportunity for a Host to drive additional 500+ trips from Kenny.

We often focus on personal skills in Player Development and many Hosts will say 'Oh, I am not a numbers person' but, in reality, the Strategic Host thinks about the intricacies and challenges of crafting an effective Direct Mail program and the appropriate criteria for who to code and why.

Offers and Comps

Learn how to view the offers inside the system and to decode what they mean. (It won't say $50 in Free Slot Play in June; it will say something cryptic like SP 50 06 CP1234 which means Free Slot Play, $50, the sixth month i.e. June, and the coupon number.)

If you can view the offers, you can mention them in an outbound phone call to attract the player in for a trip. "Hey Beth, I see you have $100 in free play next week, let's get you in?"

You can also use the offers to avoid making comps. If the guest has hotel coupons that haven't yet been redeemed, you can offer to make the hotel reservation for them using the coupon.

Can you make comps? Do you have discretion in what to offer your best players?

If so, don't over invest. When the guest asks for a comp'd steakhouse reservation, look at their offers and decide if the comp is warranted on top of the other offers they might redeem during the trip.

If they've got an offer for two show tickets and they ask for four seats, look at recent play to see if the add-on is warranted. (Maybe they had a big loss since the mailer went out?)

Remember to look at spouse play or other mitigating factors (how frequently they customarily visit, whether they likely visit competitor properties, recent illnesses or bad weather etc.) in your calculations.

And always make a note of how and why you made your decision! (Even if this is not a Comp Exception).

What is a Comp Exception?

Management will create a Comp Matrix which is a set of rules, usually in a MS Excel spreadsheet, about who can get what kind of comp, and who can approve an override. E.g. perhaps only a VP can approve a comp for alcohol in the steakhouse.

A Comp Exception means that someone has approved a comp that the guest did not qualify for, or that broke the rules of the Comp Matrix. The Finance/Audit team will be monitoring the comps to check for fraud or wastage, and you can expect to be asked about decisions that you made days and weeks ago. Hence it is always a good idea to make a note about your logic and who approved it.

If managers and the Finance/Audit team can read your note when they study the numbers, then they won't come back and waste your time with questions about the past.

Sound Business Decisions

You work for the casino, but the players provide the dollars in your paycheck. It can create a balancing act for you, because often what the player wants is at odds with what the company says you can provide, and you have to make sound business decisions.

"Ensure that you know what the company expects of your position. And that you know the difference between a profitable and non-profitable guest.

Learn the financial side of the business instead of completely focusing on being the host that all the players like the best. That is usually a sign that you just say yes to every request and require someone else to clean up the mess.

The easiest way to lose a guest to your competition is to set their expectations too high because at some point, someone will need to step in and try to get them back to profitable for the organization."

In this quote, the VP is alluding to the reality that Executives will 'fire' your player if they are unprofitable for the casino because, although they play well, they take full advantage of every offer, comp, event, and they drink all of the best liquor in the VIP lounge. They will cut the player off with the intention that this unwanted guest goes to the competition and drinks them dry instead.

Making sound business decisions is the hallmark of a good casino host. Always balance the guest's needs with the company's success. Paying a player to patronize your casino is never a good idea because you haven't actually secured their loyalty at an emotional level.

If you want to become a Player Development Executive and have your own list then you need those solid emotional connections because, as you move from Property to Property, you won't have the same ability to give away 'stuff'.

And if you want to proceed into management then you absolutely have to demonstrate a grasp of the financial side of PD.

Breaking and Making Rules

It should be your last resort to bend or break a rule. Once you've broken a rule to accommodate a guest's wishes, you've actually established a new rule.

The guest will likely expect a similar accommodation in the future even after you tactfully communicated to him that this was a one-time only situation.

Worse, the other players will hear about the special favor you've done for John, and they are likely to ask you for similar treatment because they are in the same situation as John was. What are you going to say then? If you refuse, then you are implying that they are not as important as the other guest and you will hear this rude retort: "Oh, I see, the rule is that we can get the upgrade if our name is John."

People get very upset when they think you are not being fair. Bending and breaking the rules is a slippery slope, so it's probably best to avoid the trip down the hill.

Become a Walking Encyclopedia

There is another way in which you can help your guests and that doesn't cost anything other than your time and attention.

You can know your Property inside and out; all of the restaurants all of the retail outlets, and all of the amenities. The opening times, the average wait time, the specials, and today's offers. You need to be able to rave about the garlic mushrooms at the steak-house or your favorite flavor of morning muffin at the coffee shop.

Turn yourself into a walking encyclopedia so you can answer every question plus up-sell and cross-sell. Does Bill want a burger? Can you **up-sell** him from a burger at the café into a rib-eye at the steakhouse? His wife, Robin, does not gamble and wants to go into the city. Can you **cross-sell** a spa appointment instead?

You can also study the details of all the Events and Promotions. What time is the Ham Giveaway and where will it be? When is the Chinese New Year's party and who is the entertainment?

This approach will save you time because you can immediately answer questions without making a call or looking at the casino website. It will also position you to gather information because you can slide right into asking questions about preferences and social connections.

Let's imagine you are walking the Casino Floor, and your best player, Tomas, is approaching with three friends. You give Tomas a big welcoming smile and slow your pace. He asks you about the High Limit room and what time the live music starts in the bar next door.

With smooth confidence, you reply "The live music starts at six. Are you all going to be playing with Tomas? Hi, I don't think we've met…"

And then Tomas introduces you to his high-roller friends who are visiting your Casino for the first time, and you are making some valuable new connections.

It is a good practice to always accompany the guest to their destination. As you walk to the High Limit room with Tomas and his friends, you have a few more precious minutes to build the relationships by asking open questions about their lives and their preferences. This also demonstrates that you will literally go out of your way for Tomas, and it makes him feel important in front of his friends.

When you go out on the casino floor, think of yourself as the proud owner of the entire Property, and that you are happy to have these guests in your 'home'.

Always Follow Through

This may seem like a no brainer, but it needs to be stated clearly: don't drop the ball! (And when you do, own it and fix it as quickly and painlessly as possible. It will happen. Everyone makes mistakes.)

Whether it's a reservation confirmation, the answer to an inquiry, or simply a reply to a guest communication, make your responses timely and accurate. Don't leave your players waiting or guessing. Instill confidence in your service by being on top of the details and communicating them to the pertinent patron. Being dependable is one of your biggest assets.

> "As a player's host, you are his 'inside man.' You should be able to get him a room or dinner reservations or show tickets or registration for a tournament or other event without him having to do more than ask you to take care of it.
>
> Afterward, **relentless follow-up** is required. Always return a guest's call as soon as humanly possible and always do what you say you will do. If you're making reservations, call back with a confirmation that the task is complete, no matter whether the reservation is for today or in three weeks."

Everyone in Player Development has to follow through for their guests if they want to build the vital trust that underlies any relationship.

You might enjoy reading the book *Six Habits of Effective People*. The author, Stephen Covey, uses the metaphor of an Emotional Bank Account to describe "the amount of trust that's been built up in a relationship". Simply put, if I do five favors for my neighbors then I have made five deposits in my emotional bank account with them. If I mess up and reverse into their mailbox, I have to make a large withdrawal! But, if I had never done any favors then I would have gone over-drawn. If you are consistent with your follow-through then your guest will forgive you if you make a mistake. (The same applies with your manager and your peers. Keep making deposits in those emotional bank accounts and you will have a cushion in your favor for when you make mistakes.)

Happy to be with People!

Being a Casino Host is a physically demanding role because of the long hours, shift-work, being on your feet and on your 'game' for the entire shift, and varied duties all across the property.

It is also an emotionally exhausting role if it doesn't fit your personality! An **introvert** can appear to be very out-going but interacting with guests for 8 hours will drain them; whereas an **extrovert** will be on a high from all of those conversations and new people!

If you have not heard the terms Extrovert and Introvert, do some research because it will give you more insight into yourself and also the different personalities of your guests.

Extroverts increase their energy when interacting with others. Introverts lose energy when interacting with others and re-charge in solitude. And a loud out-going person is not necessarily an Extrovert.

As a player development professional, you know that everyone is different and yet so many people seem to fall into certain 'types'.

From your practical experience dealing with guests, you know that some people need excruciating details why they cannot have an upgrade and other people are happy with your simple 'No'. Some types of people get very emotional with you about the change to the Buffet, and other people will tell you in a flat monotone voice that they have just lost a loved one.

As you go through your shift, you adjust to the different personality types and clearly see how they adjust and react to the world around them. It is not about how you see the situation, it is about how they see the situation.

Have you ever taken a personality test? Myers Briggs is a widely used example. Not that any one of these personality models is absolute but you will learn more about how different people absorb information in different ways and react in different ways. Follow the link down below to see a lovely illustration of the 16 personality types in the Myers Briggs model.

Why would you care? Well, for two reasons. As a player development professional, you specialize in influencing human behavior (which we call 'sales') and so you need to study people with a passion. And a business professional, you have to interact with your manager, and with your peers. If you know yourself, and you realize that not everyone sees the world the same way, then you will be more open to others and experience less stress.

We often think of a personality test as describing the person but we are really exploring how they perceive the world and make decisions. In player development, we need to know how people perceive their world and make decisions on where to play, what to play, how long to play, and why to play.

The Myers–Briggs Type Indicator classifies people in four dimensions. For example, I am classified as an INTJ. Here is what this means to you, if I am your coded player:

I – Introversion. INTJ expend energy interacting with people in social situations (whereas extroverts gain energy). In the Casino, I don't want to spend a lot of time with you. I am happily alone at the slots trying to recharge from a day of dealing with others. Say Hi but don't hang around. (You might not relate! You are probably an Extrovert.)

N – Intuition preferred to sensing: INTJs tend to be more abstract than concrete. They focus their attention on the big picture rather than the details and on future possibilities rather than immediate realities. This means that I 'get it' when you say No.

T – Thinking preferred to feeling: INTJs tend to value objective criteria above personal preference or sentiment. When making decisions they generally give more weight to logic than to social considerations. So I won't get all emotional with you. I won't take your Comp decisions personally if they 'make sense' to me.

J – Judgment preferred to perceiving. INTJs tend to approach life in a structured way, planning and organizing their world to achieve their goals. This means I want to know how to get what I want; tell me how to get to Platinum.

It costs money to take the official Myers Briggs test but you can try one for free at sites like this one www.16personalities.com

Go online and take a test and see if you agree with what it says about you! **I place a large bet that you are an ES-something: a Consul, Entertainer, or an Entrepreneur.** But if you are an I-something then you might be in the wrong profession because people will wear you down as an introvert!

As a player development professional, you need to be an expert in human behavior. You probably would not be reading this book if you didn't understand people intuitively, but it always helps to research.

Speaking of psychology, some of your guests enjoy the thrill of seeing what they can get out of you today. They will throw the biggest scene necessary to try to get you to fold and give them what they want.

"A sensitive person will fail in player development. You have to have a thick skin because guests will get upset and guests will yell at you. It happens. So, you have to be the kind of person that can focus on the good things and realize that this bad moment won't last. If you don't have a thick skin, you will drop out."

You have to be calm and polite with a backbone made of steel because the players have tactics to try to break you.

They might try **blackmail** you with *I was next door at competition and the Host over there gave me X and if you can't do it then I am going over there.*

They might try to **bully** you *This is not fair. My friend got one. I know your grandmother, I've been coming every day for years and this is your best? I gave you that sports team cap last week.*

And they might try to **bluff** you with *Well you clearly don't understand the program because my play is well above the criteria if you look at it properly. Let me talk to someone who knows what they are doing.*

Finally, they will resort to **shopping** with each Host just as a kid goes from Mum to Dad to try get approval for the ice-cream.

Be an iron fist inside a kid glove

Your overall appearance (the kid glove) is that of a warm, open, caring person. But if I try to roll over you with my demands then I will find that you are smiling and un-bending (the iron fist) and I won't be able to bend you.

'The effective Host is tough but gentle with their words"

Be careful that you don't become jaded and start to generalize. Each player is different. If someone has been pushing your buttons to get a free comp, don't immediately shut down the next person as also being 'on-the-make.'

Always Be Happy To Help!

Self-Assessment

Before you read on, grab a pen and complete this self-assessment. Where are your areas for improvement?

Skill	Always	Most of the time	Rarely
I focus on making a connection and not an offer.			
I educate my guests on what they have to do, to get what they want.			
I am careful to say No without causing offence, hurting feelings, or appearing unfair.			
I understand the Points levels and the detailed benefits of the Club.			
I nurture my relationship with Direct Mail to avoid surprises.			
I keep track of the offers and I promote them to my guests.			
I walk the guest to their destination.			
I am an iron fist in a kid glove.			
I have a passion for Player Development!			

5 ways to help people to immediately warm to you.

We all judge people on our first impression of them. So here are five ways to help people to immediately warm to you.

In your mind, assume that you are going to really like this person, and that they are going to like you. This is the "Fake it till you can make it" approach. And it works, because your positive attitude will influence all of the following techniques.

The new person will sense that you are approaching them with openness and warmth, and they will respond. This is called the *reciprocity of liking*. If the guest believes that you like them, then they will like you back!

Smile! This is such an old-fashioned recommendation but so true. When the guest sees your smile, they see your warmth, your openness, and your welcome.

But it needs to be a real smile that shines in your eyes as well. This only happens if you adopt Rule #1 which is that, in your mind, you have already decided that you like this person, and so you are smiling in anticipation of enjoying talking with them.

Even if you are playing the role of the Negative Enforcer, such as 'No, You Cannot Have That Comp', you can still approach them with a smile. It does not give away your power, it actually makes you seem in control and gracious.

Compliment! As you walk towards this guest, find something that you can compliment. The way their shoes match their outfit? Their funky baseball cap? You are off to a good start if you can ask a question such as "I love that purse, where did you find it?" If you cannot find anything then take a quick look at the people with them! If their friend has a Boston t-shirt then start out with "I loved Boston. The lobster is amazing!"

This approach is called *Spontaneous Trait Transference*! This fancy term means that people will assume that YOU have the same qualities with which you describe others. If you are saying nice, kind, generous, enthusiastic things about other people, then the listener will assume that you are kind, generous, enthusiastic etc. If you cannot think of anything to say about them, then have some general phrases all ready to go such as 'What a great atmosphere in here tonight, everyone is having so much fun!" You are saying something positive, so they will assume that you are a positive person.

We like positive people because we assume that they will put up with us and our quirks!

Copy! There are very subtle ways for you to copy the Guest. If they are wearing a team-shirt then you can bond over sports. You can match their body language e.g. leaning sideways into a slot machine. Don't mimic their accent but you can slightly copy their tone and speed of speech. This is called *mirroring* and the concept is that the guest will relax with you if you seem to be like them.

You can also repeat their phrases and observations back to them. If they say, "I can't believe the buffet has run out of crab legs", you reply "I can't believe that either. It just shows how much everybody loves it. I guess you do too. Do you eat all kinds of seafood?"

In that simple response, you first copy their phrase (can't believe), you give a positive spin (everybody loves it), and then you turn it around to them (and try to change the subject!)

Extract and Repeat Some Facts! Everybody wants to be 'seen' and acknowledged. Develop a range of open questions that you can use to smoothly get them to talk about themselves.

"Hi, I am Kim. I wanted to introduce myself and see if you are having a wonderful time here today. Are you having fun?" You can ask where they are from, you can ask what they enjoy most about the property, and you can ask for their opinion on anything new such as an Amenity or an event.

Before you walk away, be sure to repeat back some of what you have learned, along with their name. "Well Carol, I hope you have a safe drive back to Charlotte, and you come and see us the next time you visit your son Harry. Have a great day, and perhaps you will be back to see us before you leave on Tuesday?"

That closing line tells them that you truly paid attention!

Chapter 4. O IS FOR ORGANIZED

"It's about doing a little bit today
so that tomorrow is a little easier for you."
Alison Kero

You won't spot the organized host because their desk is tidier than everyone else. It might be! But not necessarily.

This is how you recognize the organized host! Can you check all the boxes for yourself?

- ☐ Your guests never complain to management.

- ☐ You meet or exceed all of your KPIs. Always.

- ☐ Your VIP parties and Host events always run smoothly and make a profit.

- ☐ You never miss a deadline and management never has to ask twice.

- ☐ You arrive 2 minutes early for team meetings and you are calm and composed. You have even read the agenda!

- ☐ You somehow find the time to have relaxed conversations with guests. You don't run around the property with your head cut off.

- ☐ You make it all look easy!

Life is much easier when you are organized because you don't have the added stress of cleaning up your own mess. You deal with everything just once and put it behind you.

If a guest calls in and requests the limo then you send an email to your Manager as soon as you hang up; you don't write yourself a note, stick it your monitor, and deal with it later.

If you have to complete a shift report and you know that it takes ten minutes, then you set a timer on your phone for twenty minutes before the end of your shift, and you get it done. If a guest calls in while you are writing, then it doesn't matter because you scheduled extra time.

If you run a VIP party, then you make a list of everything that has to be done. After the event, you keep the list, a copy of the invitation, a copy of the email, and even the menu. When you run the next VIP party, you pull out the files from last time and you don't have to start from scratch.

If a guest complains about their offers, then you immediately send an email to Direct Marketing with the name, account number, and their complaint. You cc: yourself and put the email into a folder called Offer Complaints. If the guest comes back to you then you can easily find your email and assure them you followed up.

If you have any kind of Host software, then you know all of the features and you use them to your advantage. The software reminds you to call Mary because it is her birthday, it reminds you that Sasha is arriving today for a weekend trip, and it warns you that Ishmael has not played for a month.

Key Principles

There are some key principles in all of these examples:

1. **Touch everything just once!** When something comes up, deal with it right away or give it to someone else to solve. If you cannot delegate it, and it will take some time, then put it on your calendar and forget about it until then. Yes, literally schedule 30 minutes on your calendar to write that report for your boss.

2. **Move the Monkey!** This is a great visual. If someone gives you a problem to solve then imagine that they have put a monkey on your back. Too many monkeys and you will feel crushed. So, as soon as possible, move that monkey onto

someone else's back! That said, make a note to yourself to follow up. You own the Monkey even when it is off your back.

"Follow up and follow through: Simple. Always follow up with your players and follow through on what you promise. If a problem or task falls on your desk, follow it through until the end…especially if it involves incorporating other people. Don't assume because you have passed it off or sent an email that it is completed. Follow up on the request and follow through on the delivery. Every time."

3. **Don't start from scratch.** Whenever you do anything, assume that you are going to have to do it again and again and again! Organized people are actually very lazy people; they want it to be easier the next time, and they assume that there will be a next time. So, they keep all the information about how they arranged that VIP party. And they keep the memo from Accounts on how to resolve an obscure refund for a guest because what happens once, will happen again.

4. **Put Things Where You Will Find Them.** In your email, create folders labeled 'Comp Exception', 'Refund Dispute', 'Limo Request' and 'How to Use Systems'. Drag emails into the folders and out of the in-box. Your in-box should only contain your current Monkeys that you are going to quickly move along before the shift ends.

In your phone, keep the numbers for Guest Services, Front Desk, Housekeeping supervisor, and that helpful person in Accounts who can approve Portfolio adjustments.

And your desk does not have to be tidy, but each leaning stack of papers should contain related items!

If you take these steps, you will gain time and energy and be better able to meet and exceed your KPIs. It will also help you get promoted because Senior management will assume that you can handle additional responsibilities. In contrast, if Management sees a Host struggling to stay on top of their current responsibilities then they are certainly not going to promote them and give them more challenges!

So, how do you make the change?

Stop thinking about being organized as having a permanently clean and tidy home. It will never happen. Every day, you have to clean your body, feed the cat, prepare some meals, and brush your teeth. It is an endless cycle. In the same way, you accept that when you come to work, you are going to repeat the same tasks over and over again so, being essentially lazy, the Organized Host will try to make it easier and easier to issue the comp, track the hotel reservation, follow up on the dispute, and book the limo.

You constantly look for ways to make the everyday tasks be easier. You decide to watch and learn from organized people. And you keep reading!

> "Never let 'em see you sweat! Even when you're running around the casino like a madman on a Saturday night, take your time to walk through the gaming areas, keeping in mind that the guests may take a cue from your behavior.
>
> Walk with a purpose, but like you own the place. Even when you're on your way to a firefight, take advantage of opportunities to briefly "touch" players you know and make a mental note to get back to them when you have a moment. Be calm and plan your next move instead of being buffeted by the tides of a busy casino floor.
>
> Better yet, plan your day ahead of time. Build in a buffer to accommodate the unexpected, and you'll accomplish more."

Remember, organized people are actually lazy! They figure out how to complete repetitive tasks with a lot less effort and a lot more results.

Daily Practices

Here are some specific recommendations for you to follow on a daily basis.

- **Keep a list**. On paper, in a MS Excel spreadsheet, in software, whatever. Do not keep your tasks on stickies on your monitor.

  Maintain one task list for work, and a second task list for your personal life with items that you need to complete during the working day, such as Call Dentist, Book flights, and File Taxes.

  Many Player Development professionals are so focused on their job that they lose track of what needs to be completed in their personal lives.

- **Plan Your Day.** At the start of your shift, pull out your two lists and study them. Grab a new piece of paper and write Today on it. Pick **3** tasks that you will definitely get done today and write them on the Today list. Put the other two lists away until tomorrow. Yes, until tomorrow.

  Why only pick 3 tasks? Because you are going to have a million other tasks come your way during the day, and you need to leave room for them. If, by some miracle, you get to the end of your shift with nothing to do, then you can pull out those lists and do more! What is more likely, is that you will fight to even finish the 3 but you will have a great sense of satisfaction when you do.

  Look at your calendar for any commitments. And then plan your day around your commitments. When will you place those 10 tele-marketing phone calls about the up-coming event? 10 calls at 3 minutes each means you need to find a 30 minute block. How about right now, before you go down to the casino floor?

  At 7pm you will be standing around backstage in case the Band needs anything. Who could you call from back-stage and not waste that time?

Your job involves a lot of unexpected calls and situations, so you obviously cannot plan the whole shift down to the minute; but if you don't make a general plan then you will not get everything done.

- **Swallow the Frog!** Isn't that disgusting? It means you first do the ugliest, nastiest, task and get it out of the way.

  Call that unhappy guest. Tell your boss that you went outside the Comp Matrix. Speak to the Accounting department about that credit application that you don't messed up.

- *"No amount of guilt can change the past, and no amount of worrying can change the future."*
  Umar Ibn Al-Khattaab

Swallow the frog! This will give you confidence in your self-discipline! And it will free you up from worrying about that task and procrastinating.

- **Group your activities**. If you are calling four people to wish them Happy Birthday, then try to do that back to back. If you are calling eight people to remind them about the concert, then try to do that back to back. You will be much more efficient if you complete similar activities at one time, because your mind will be 'in that groove'.

  That said, you need to know the preferences of your guests. Can you catch them in the morning or do you have to wait for the afternoon? If you don't pay attention to their preference, then you will end up with a lot of un-answered calls and texts and have to repeat the effort. Remember – **organized people are actually lazy people** and don't want to duplicate effort!

- **Create scripts.** If you are calling about a concert, then note down the key points that you want to make and in which order. If you get the guest, or leave a voicemail, you will be ready with a fluent message.

- **Create email templates.** Yes, you must tailor each email to the individual, but you can start with a template, a default email for each of 'Happy Birthday', 'Great to meet you', 'Where have you been'? If you don't know how to make a template, then get on Youtube!

  You should also create internal email templates as well such as 'Please make a dinner reservation at Steakhouse for account X on this day, this time, this number of people". You click on the template, type the account number, date, time, and number of people, and hit send.

- We talked before about **carrying a Calendar** for the events and promotions. Make friends with the Marketing Coordinator and have them send it to you. Preferably as a real calendar that you can load to your phone or into your Host CRM.

  Review the Marketing Calendar each morning so you know the details and you can quickly answer any questions from your guests.

- **Be prepared.** Part of your job is to introduce yourself to new players and encourage them to enroll. Along with your business card, can you carry a simple summary of club benefits?

- **Leverage others.** Make friends with the Front Desk so when your guest checks in, they give them an envelope with your business card, and a standard letter that says 'Welcome. Give me a call or text at 1234 when you have settled in. I look forward to catching up with you!" This saves you from having to hover around Reception.

- Schedule time at the end of your shift to **review the next day**. What is on your calendar for tomorrow? Which guests are arriving and when? What did you have to push from today to tomorrow and when will you get it done? Do you need to come in a little earlier? You will never walk out of the building feeling that you have done everything. But you can walk out of the building feeling happy that you have everything under control.

- Take a **Two Minute Tidy** at the end of your shift. Straighten up your papers, put away the pens, throw away your trash, and take that nasty coffee cup to the kitchen. When you walk in tomorrow, you will be impressed at your own self-discipline and you will feel emboldened.

If you adopt these practices, and learn more from the people around you, then I promise that you will have less stress, feel more confident, and impress your boss.

> "Hosts must be consistent! Being consistent makes others around you feel comfortable and know they can depend on you. Consistent in your delivery, your offerings, your follow through. You don't ever want a player to feel unsure about a reservation you said you would make or tickets you said you would get."

It is stressful enough being a Host. You don't need to add to your own stress by dropping the ball and having to invest time in recovering the situation.

While interviewing managers for this book, they emphasized that Casino Hosts must be detail oriented and follow through for the guest.

> "A host must be organized on a day-to-day basis and not lose track of their guest's needs. If you mess up and lose their trust, they'll find a replacement (potentially from a different property). Hosts must understand that their actions represent much more than just themselves. They are present in most of their guests' experience, as they influence almost every aspect; From dining, resort, promotions, special events, to membership, Hosts have a hand in literally everything. It's imperative that they are always on the ball."

The Organized Host knows their own weaknesses and take steps to overcome them. If you tend to let your phone calls run too long, then set a timer. If you procrastinate then write Swallow the Frog on your monitor! The details don't matter; what's important is that you continually find ways to increase your productivity and reduce your stress.

Your beliefs become your thoughts,
Your thoughts become your words,
Your words become your actions,
Your actions become your habits,
Your habits become your values,
Your values become your destiny.

— Mahatma Gandhi

Self-Assessment

Before you read on, grab a pen and complete this self-assessment. Where are your areas for improvement?

Skill	Always	Most of the time	Rarely
My manager thinks of me as organized			
I am one of the first people to arrive for a meeting			
My manager thinks of me as following through on every detail			
If I arrange to meet a guest at 6pm then I will arrive at 5:57pm			
I plan my day.			
I 'touch things once'			
I save time with templates and scripts and other techniques.			
In my personal life, I stay on top of bills, appointments etc.			
I keep a healthy work-life balance			

Get that Glow! (The Healthy Host)

It's not enough to put on a smart outfit. You need the attractive healthy glow that comes from a healthy life-style.

If you are under 30 then you probably assume you will feel this energetic forever but unfortunately that is not true! Your long-term success and personal health will be dictated by the habits that you form now.

Do you find yourself doing nothing but work and sleep? If you let yourself become obsessed, then your stress level will go up and it will interfere with your judgement. If you don't make a change, you will lose perspective, make poor decisions, and look and feel pale and sickly. So, plan your down-time and organize your life as well as your job.

Plan to rest! Part of being organized is to come up with ways to ensure you regularly disconnect, rest, and re-charge. You love what you do, and your job can easily be a 24-hour business for seven days a week. But you can burn-out and you certainly won't deliver your best if you are exhausted.

Plan on having a meal even a quick one. Skipping meals and trying to survive on sugar and caffeine will destroy your productivity and problem-solving skills. It also affects your waistline!

Plan to get outside and get some air and sunshine. Can you walk around the outside patios, greet some guests and catch some rays?

Eat your fruits and vegetables! It can be hard to 'eat well' when you are running around all day long and working difficult hours. But try to have something fresh with each meal; or make salads in mason jars on your day off and take a salad each day.

Drink lots of water to keep your skin hydrated. Is water boring? Then find something that makes it palatable like adding some lemon juice.

By the way, coffee dehydrates you. I realize you might need the caffeine to get going but **peppermint** is a good alternative for a pick me up because Mint stimulates the brain. Plus, peppermint is more pleasant than coffee breathe!

Build **movement** into your daily routine. Park the furthest away from the building, park at the top of the parking garage and use the staircase to get up there at the end of your shift, and always use a staircase instead of an elevator. Use the restroom on a different floor of the building and use the steps to get there.

Find a way to **disconnect** for as little as 20 minutes a day; leave the phone behind and go for a walk, go to the gym, listen to a motivational video, soak in the bath, or read an interesting novel. Set the timer on your phone for 20 minutes and then don't touch that phone until it goes off. You will be amazed how long 20 minutes will feel!

Take your vacations! I promise you that your peers can take care of your players. You are not indispensable. You need to get away for a week at a time to re-charge.

As the saying goes 'All work and no play make Jack a dull boy!'

Chapter 5. THE ORGANIZED EVENT

"To achieve great things, two things are needed: a plan and not quite enough time." Leonard Bernstein

In this chapter, we provide a blue-print for organizing an event such as a Chinese New Years party, or a Valentines Day Ball.

As a **new** Host, you will be asked to make out-bound calls and invite the guests, and to attend the actual event and welcome the guests. Read this chapter so that you understand the entire process and how you fit in.

As an **experienced** Host, you arrange VIP Parties on a smaller scale but following these same principles, so you will find this chapter to be invaluable.

If your career aspiration is to move into Management then helping to run these Events will give you an introduction to advertising, direct marketing, entertainment, operations, and more. You won't get paid more to volunteer to help but you will gain an invaluable education.

And finally, use this Chapter to think carefully about your own Casino. Are there ideas in here that you could recommend to management? It is always good to position yourself as someone making helpful suggestions – as long as you come over as creative and not as critical!

(Kayle McKenzie generously provided the bulk of this Chapter. Thank you, Kayle.)

Let's start at the beginning with the creation of a pro-forma to build a business case and obtain approval from management.

Pro-Forma

The pro-forma is a short description of the proposed event along with an estimate of the profit (or loss) by anticipating all the expenses and calculating the expected income from the players. This is usually done in MS Excel and of course the Organized Host will keep these and not start from scratch each time.

Here is a brief example:

Event:	Chinese New Year	**Date:**	Feb 5th		
Description:	By invitation event, RSVP required, with additional free tickets available				
	based on guest worth. Includes food, cash bar, entertainment, and				
	free play. Runs from 8 to 10:30. Free drink, hor d'ouevres, and ticket pickup from 5pm				
	The intention is to have guests arrive and play from 5pm onwards.				
	Chinese dragon will be on casino floor between 5pm and 8pm.				
Expenses		Revenue			
Mailer		Estimated slot play:			
Advertizing		Estimated table play:			
Decoration					
Entertainment					
Free play					
Free drink					
Food					
Extra servers					
Extra security					
Extra valets					
Total Expense:		Total Revenue:			
Total Profit:					

On the left, we make a list of all the expenses and we take a guess at the cost for transportation, food, drink, tickets, staffing, and hotel rooms, etc. On the right, we have an estimate of the revenue from extra slot play and extra table play.

Profit = Revenue - Expense

To estimate the play (the Revenue) we work with the Database team to figure out who will be invited, based on ADT, and how much they might play before, during, and after the Event. E.g. Inviting 100 people with an ADT 500+ might generate 100 x 500 = 5,000. You are usually trying to generate a profit, so you invite people based on their ADT and you assume you will to add a Trip.

In complete contrast, you might have a box at a major sporting event, offsite, so you decide to invite, and reward, the players who have contributed the most in the current year. Your criteria would be total Actual Loss. But you would still like an extra trip, so you require them to pick up their tickets at the Casino the night before! PD is sneaky like that…

Planning

Create a list of all the tasks that you can possibly think of, from sending the invitations, to booking the entertainment, to making sure there is extra security on the night.

	OWNER	DUE-DATE	STATUS	NOTES
PLANNING AND APPROVAL				
Finish pro-format				
Sign off with CFO				
Sign off with compliance				
PROMOTE AND INVITE				
Design invitation				
Design advertizing				
Change website				
Prepare Guest Services				
Create RSVP process				
Pull list				
Send invitations				
Ask Hosts to call				
PLAN EVENT				
Book room				
Decide menu				
Book entertainer				
Book dragon				
Schedule security				
Schedule valets				

Share the plan across the team and make sure everyone understands their specific tasks. Who creates the invites? Who communicates with the artwork team? Who sets up the parameters for the event?

Make sure that you are sharing all of the details with all the right people, including the Host team, the Guest Services team, the Security team, and more. Provide a regular update to management on how many people are confirmed and don't wait until too late to request an additional email blast or voice-blast to drive up the interest.

Invitations

The invitations can be via email, text, or mailer. It depends on your demographic. The date, time, and location should be easy to see. Ask someone else to proof-read the invitation to make sure you have not made a mistake. If you are using any kind of images, then allow plenty of time for the design to be created and approved.

Management approved "fine print" should be included with every invite, such as "Cannot be combined with any other offer. Subject to availability."

Generating the List

The mailing list will be pulled by the Database Team following the criteria that were decided earlier on while creating the pro-forma.

(Back when we were designing the event, the Database team was pulling an initial list to count numbers such as 'How many people have this ADT and live in these zip-codes and are coded as Asian?' Now, the Database Team is pulling the actual list.)

Remove guests from the list if they habitually let you down. You drop these people to create room to invite other players who might actually show up. Work with your manager on criteria such as 'people are dropped if they have been a no show/cancel for every event in the last 3 months.' If the person complains that they did not receive an invitation, then you have the perfect opportunity to modify their behavior. You explain that they have been a no show/cancel, then mark them as a definite invitation for the next event and see what happens.

Manage the RSVPs

Before you send out the mailer, make sure you have created a way to manage the RSVPs and you have informed any casino employee who might receive a response from a player. This could include the Host team, the Players Club Ambassadors, and the Guest Services team that answer the phones.

You need to have a detailed master guest list to keep track of all the information: Guest name, Account Number, Number of tickets, Host name etc.

And you need a way to keep track of all the different scenarios:

- Guest is not coming.
- Guest confirmed for 2 people.
- Guest called back and requested 3 people.
- Guest canceled.

This is often done in a shared MS Excel file and it can become a mess! One person should oversee the RSVP process to ensure accuracy and clarity. As a Host, you should keep track of your own bookings and cancellations in case the shared spreadsheet becomes corrupt!

Manage your Occupancy

Managing your tickets and hotel rooms is a big challenge! You have a fixed number of tickets and a fixed number of hotel rooms. You cannot give away more than you have but you don't them to go un-used.

Recommend that your Casino keeps track of the average response rate for all events, so you can base your guess on prior events. For example, what happened at VIP Chinese New Year last year, the year before you arrived?

Let's say your property has a 15% no show/cancel rate. If you book 180 people, and 15% don't show up, you have $180 \times 0.15 = 27$ no-shows and you cannot meet your estimate for Actual from just $180-27 = 153$ players.

Instead take the same approach as the airlines and overbook! You might decide it is safe to overbook by 20 and you book 200. If you invite 200 and 15% don't show, then $200 * 0.15 = 30$ do not attend and you have $200 - 30 = 170$ players

As you can imagine, it requires experience and courage to overbook, and you would be greatly helped by keeping track of what has happened at past events.

"This chair is too big!" Goldilocks exclaimed. She sat in the second chair. "This chair is too big, too!". She tried the last chair. "Ahhh this chair is just right" she sighed.

Manage your hotel rooms.

Some events require more King or Queen rooms than others. Once you start booking, you will get a feel for what the event requires. Save the rooms you know you will use and let the hotel sell the rooms you know you won't use.

(As a Host, you might have good intentions in saving rooms for your guests but if you habitually have multiple un-booked rooms, it is lost revenue and will reflect badly on you.)

Do not allow your hosted guests to book multiple comped rooms on a show night. The hosted guest will play less if they are with a large party because they will want to be social. Plus, their guests are mostly likely not high playing gamers, or they would have their own comped room in the first place! Show nights should be busy with a packed house. You want as many VIP gamers as possible.

Final confirmations

Confirming your guests is a top priority. It can often be a long time between the booking and the actual event.

As a Host, this gives you the perfect reason to make an out-bound call and touch base with your players and keep up the relationship.

It is also a really good idea to re-qualify the guest and make sure that they are coming. If they don't commit, then you are better to record them as a cancellation and not get dinged later that your guests are no cancel/no show.

Check In Process

As people arrive for the Event, they have to go through some kind of check-in process. This needs to be a very organized and fast process. It sets the tone for the evening. The guest has arrived feeling excited and you don't want them to become annoyed by a long line.

Besides! You want them gaming and not standing in line.

As the Host, work with Marketing and the Players Club to be clear on 'who is doing what'. Hopefully the Host is walking the line and greeting the guests, and a different department is handling the check-in process.

As the Host, you welcome each guest and ask if they have any questions You can describe the food options, handle the concerns about the parking deck, and explain what to do if the guest has forgotten their invitation. This will speed up the check-in process.

If a guest has an issue, ask them to come talk with you away from the line. Assure them they have not lost their place, but you want to discuss their matter one on one, with your undivided attention. This keeps the line moving.

The guest should spend no more than a few minutes actually checking in, because the Hosts have intercepted all of the questions. Here are some tips on a smooth check-in process. You can use these tips for VIP parties as well:

- Make your check in window/stand/table is clearly marked with proper signage.

- Offer a priority check in for the highest tiered guests. You want them back on the floor, and you also want the other guests to see the benefit of moving up the club.

- Have everything you are handing the guest (tickets, drink coupons, prizes) in one envelope and pre-packaged.

- Beforehand, ask the other Hosts to go through and put their card in the right envelopes.

- Use technology to check-in but have several print outs of your guest list in case technology fails!

Gifts and Special Treatment

If you are going to give a gift, be thoughtful about how this will appear to the other guests. You are not going to treat all of the guests equally, not even all of the VIPs, and you don't want people to get upset about what they didn't receive. If you give free play, then hand-out an attractive envelope with the amount printed on a card inside so people cannot easily see what everyone else has received. Don't make it obvious that some people are receiving lavish expensive gifts.

Are you going to let people sit first-come first-served? It is hard work to arrange pre-assigned seats, but it does let you place the VIP guests in the preferred setting. There are lots of logistical challenges including, for example, you don't always know if they are going to bring that extra guest that they are entitled to; and they might bring them even though they said they wouldn't! On the other hand, if you let people sit anywhere then two things can happen that you don't want. Your best players might get stuck in a corner and be offended. Or your players might line up early to ensure the best seats and then they are not gambling!

If you are going to treat some of the VIPs to a meet-and-greet with the entertainer, be careful that you don't make this obvious to all of your VIPs. Arrange for the lucky people to meet you in a hotel suite, out of view, or meet you at an innocuous location at a specific time and then take them from there to meet the celebrities. Don't hand out signed t-shirts or other memorabilia that the other VIPs might notice. Tell the guests that these items will be available from you when they come to play next, which might drive a trip.

You are not going to invest the same in all your players but don't make that flagrantly obvious. Don't put yourself in a situation where guests are upset because they feel were not treated fairly. They will get upset and take some, if not all, of their business elsewhere.

Follow Up

After the Event, it is all about capturing what happened and learning for next time:

- Ask the other Hosts to touch base with their guests and collect feedback.

- Copy the pro-forma, change the budgetary estimates into the actual figures, and publish the actual results as a post-forma.

- Update the plan with any extra steps for next time.

- Write a summary for management that includes lessons learned, and the post-forma.

- Make sure that everything is stored in a shared file folder so that it is available next time.

And remember to personally thank all of the different departments that helped you with the Event, be it a 500 person formal ball, or a 20 person VIP Party.

Maximize Your Dinner Party by Adding These 5 Tips

Jatonia Ziegler

As a Casino Host, your main role is to cultivate new & existing players. One of the best ways to do that is planning an exclusive dinner party for specific groups within your list of players. Your dinners should be elegantly themed, planned to perfection and managed efficiently. Your invites should be addressed to players who need that extra love and attention that will push their loyalty towards your casino. Keep in mind, not all your players need to be invited all at once.

When you're ready to plan your next dinner party at home, would you invite every single one of your friends? I'm guessing you'd be selective, I know I would. Planning a dinner for Players is no different. You need to be selective of the group you will be inviting. Think about why you're inviting them and what you'd like to accomplish during this event. Is it to gain a trip from an inactive player? Are you moving an extra visit on a day they wouldn't normally play? Will this dinner extend their stay during a trip? Find the right group to invite and then add these five tips to maximize your efforts.

Personal Invites.

Personalize it! I can't stress this enough. The first thing I learned as a host is that a "hand-written" note is the first piece of mail that is opened when grouped with bills and direct mail pieces. Make your invites stand out, put the stamp on crocked and write your guest's name in the best hand writing you have.

During one event, I wrote all my address upside down. Instead of throwing the envelopes away, I sent them out with a note saying, "Oops, turn me around"! My players loved it and found it humorous, it showed that I took the time to personally invite them and own up to a silly mistake.

Build a Team.

It may be a Player Development hosted party, but it still takes the help of other departments to pull off a success dinner party. Prior to your event, work hand in hand with the F&B Department and/or Manager of the venue you'll be using. Describe your theme and the experience you'd like your guests to have. Share tips with the staff that will "Wow" your guests, like your guest's favorite cocktail or wine. You can never be too prepared when it comes to delivering a special meal for your most valued guests.

Seating Arrangement.

Preparing and managing a large dinner party can be overwhelming, especially when you're hosting alone.

A seating arrangement is important, it can either make or break your efforts in entertaining. Two negative guests can cause an explosion that can act like a domino effect on others and you don't want that to happening.

To keep my parties fun and full of laughter, I started using placement cards and strategically place guests who played on different days yet had similar personalities and interests, near each other. Doing this, maximized my efforts in entertaining everyone all at once and gave my guests an opportunity to build new relationships with each other. Some players hit it off so well they became gambling buddies which adds extra visits to the casino and stronger loyalty.

If you can get guests to entertain each other, you can sit back and look for opportunities to cultivate new players.

Pre-set Dinner Menus.

There are two reasons why a pre-set dinner menu works best for private dinner parties for Player Development. One, it's easier on the chef and kitchen staff to prepare the meals; Two, it takes less time to serve a large party, when the menu is limited.

I suggest pre-ordering appetizers to be delivered after drinks have been served. Then limit your guests to a choice of three different entrée and two choices for dessert.

I would also recommend a pre-shift meeting with the servers working your party to explain the importance of delivering a wonderful dining experience in a fast and friendly manner. Share important information with the services about your guests that can make the dinner more special.

Design your menu to your selected theme, but don't make it too complicated that it takes away from your goal of getting your players on their favorite games immediately after dinner.

Gifts in Bags.

Gifts are a special part of a dinner party. When choosing the right gift, find one that is easy to carry, and the guest perceives as valuable.

Theme your gift to the dinner party, maybe your gift was the gorgeous centerpiece on the table or one of the special glasses that were served during dinner.

No matter what you decide to offer your guests, keep in mind that your main focus is to keep them playing for as long as you can. Offering a gift that's too large to carry or an inconvenience to keep at their favorite game, may make them walk out the door faster than you'd like. Find the right gift bag or provide an area where guests can pick up their gifts after their done playing. Make it convenient and they'll spend their time playing.

Chapter 6. S IS FOR STRATEGIC

We have been talking a lot about being organized and being efficient. But there is a big difference between being efficient and being effective! If we are efficiently doing the wrong things, then it still doesn't create results.

It is more efficient to drive a car than to ride a bicycle, but neither are effective if you are going in the wrong direction. **Efficiency** is faster/cheaper and **effective** means achieving the right results.

Walk to your goals if that is the only available transport.
Be effective not just efficient.

Being an Organized Host will make us more efficient. Being a Strategic Host will make us effective. In order to be **effective**, we have to focus on the right activities that will help us to reach our goals.

Classify Your Players

You are always going to be successful if you focus on the right players at the right time. How do you do this? The Strategic Host always classifies their players. This means that you break your player lists down into smaller groups that share something in common, like how often they play, how far away they live, and whether they play slots or tables.

Just imagine that my 300+ coded players are like a huge bag of kettle-cooked potato chips and that I pour the bag onto the table and sort them by size and shape. I really like the chips that are all folded up and crunchy, so they can go in one corner of the table. I will eat them last! I will sort the rest into four piles based on size.

If you divide your 300+ players up into smaller groups, then you will find it much easier to track their behavior and decide who you need to focus on.

Choose a set of criteria which matches your priorities. It doesn't have to be complicated. Maybe you should work on "Players within 50 miles" or "Guests who haven't been here in 31+ days" or "Ones I haven't met yet."

Classification is the process of classifying something according to shared qualities or characteristics.

If you find that you don't know much about a particular bunch of patrons, put them in the category of 'Don't Know' and start making calls to ask questions and fill in the blanks about those players.

Here is an example from an experienced Host:

> "There are guests who have just discovered your property, or maybe they just signed up for a card even though this is their 4th visit. Either way, these are your **new** players in terms of marketing.
>
> Then you have the **regulars**. These people play within a predictable pattern and are likely to be in one of the top tiers of your players club. You know them, and they know you.
>
> Surely you have **decliners** who might fall between the cracks in your player retention programs. If direct mail doesn't move them, a host call might, but if no one realizes they're missing, they might get that call too late; after they've found an alternative in one of your competitors. So, these become the ones who are **lost**. They haven't been in for a while due to reasons you may or may not know.
>
> There are decliners and lost at all levels of ADT. I really need to be aware of the decliners who are among my best players and don't let them get completely lost."

The important step is to start to think strategically about how you want to classify your players in the context of your Property and your Market. If you are a visual person, then this picture might help you:

Regular Visits High ADT	Visiting Less High ADT	Disappeared High ADT	Visiting More! Higher ADT!	New Strong Theo
Keep in regular contact.	Urgent! Find out what is happening!	Work hard at getting them back	Encourage them. Explain the Benefits.	Meet them, assess them, grow them.
Regulars	**Decliners**	**Inactive**	**Incliners**	**New**

Your **Regulars** play often with a high ADT and you just need to keep an eye on them. If they start to visit less often, or play with a lower ADT, then your revenue from them is **Declining** and you need to urgently find out what is going on. Are they mad at the change in the Buffet or the High Limit room? Has the competition thrown large amounts of Free Play at them?

If you don't find and address your Decliners, they will turn into **Inactives** which are the ghosts of what used to be a good revenue stream. You are going to have to work really hard at getting Inactives back, so it is better to catch them when they start to decline.

On a positive note, there will be people who start to visit more and play higher which means their revenue stream to you is Inclining. If you can spot the **Incliners,** then you can reach out and encourage them by giving them some extra VIP treatment. Perhaps your competition has annoyed them, and you can steal them permanently!

Finally, you want to be aware of the **newly enrolled** players with a high Theo that management has coded to you, in the hope that you can groom them into being a regular.

Like a busy sheepdog, you keep running around your pack and make sure they are all keeping up!

"A casino host should identify those players that have the potential to play big. Once they reach their highest potential they must then continue to find those middle class players to bring them up to the high level players. They should never stop looking and continue to cycle as it is a never ending position."

How do you do this? Ideally, you persuade the management team to invest in Host CRM software that does this for you, and even recommends who to call.

If you don't have Host CRM software, then ask the Database team to send you a list each week with a list of your players, the date of their last trip, and their total Theo for the last 30 days, 90 days, and 120 days. It's not easy to do in MS Excel but you can learn enough skills to find who you are looking for.

Ask someone else on your team, or ask your manager, on how to sort, Pivot, and chart your players, to find their Classification.

Types of Goals

Executive Management intuitively puts players into these kinds of classifications and they have hired you, and the rest of the Player Development team, to groom the Regulars, New, and Incliners, to track the Decliners and to prevent any In-actives.

In order to do this, Management specifies goals that you must achieve. (These are also referred to as Key Performance Indicators, KPIs)

It might sound like a burden to have to meet targets, but it is actually an advantage to you as a Host because you are then crystal clear on what you have to achieve in order to impress management and earn your promotions and perhaps bonus. Many casinos start their Player Development program by hiring one Host, without any kinds of measure, and the General Manager grumbles and regularly asks "What is person doing all day long?" So, if you are not on goals, you might want to suggest some to your Manager.

Here are two examples of goals:

The first goal is "Contact 10 Inactive players each week" so the Hosts call people that haven't played for 90 days but had high Theo when they were last playing regularly. (An organized Host will find time to call two Inactive players each day of the five-day week and 2x5=10).

And the second goal is "Bring back 20 Inactive players this quarter" so the Host has to find ways to encourage the Inactive players to return.

The first goal measures **Effort**; it measures whether you are actually trying to contact Inactive players. The second goal measures **Results**; it measures whether you are successful in getting those Inactive players back onto the Property.

There are many different types of goals. Most casinos start with Contact Goals and Active Goals.

Contact Goals measure the number of interactions that you have with your coded and un-coded players.

Active Goals aim to increase the Theo and/or Trips from Coded players e.g. *Increase total Theo by 5% over the same quarter last year.*

Inactive Goals incent you to reach out to valuable players who have not played for a while and get them back on property.

Retention Goals encourage you to monitor you Active players and ensure they do not disappear and become Inactive! If you start the quarter with 310 coded players, then 90% of them should have played at least once by the end of quarter.

New Player Goals. Newly enrolled players with high Theo are assigned to each Host. You have, say, 60 days to get the person back on property and build a pattern of play.

With **Acquisition Goals**, you try to grow trips and Theo from players who are not newly enrolled, and not yet coded to a Host, but are playing often enough, and with enough Theo, to be coded to a Host in the future.

Investment Goals measure your ability to drive trips and Theo without over-investing in the guests.

Sales Goals measure your ability to reserve hotel rooms and fill Events.

If you currently measured by goals, or you are planning to move into Management, you might want to buy our other book, *Casino Host Goals*, and learn more about this subject.

Dear General Manager,

Please talk to us, your Hosts, and you will find we face a daily dilemma regarding how to divide our time between responding to guests who are on-property and reaching out to valuable players who have not been playing.

Yes, we have an important role in providing superior customer service for the very best players when they are on-property.

This is **reactive** behavior because our team reacts to the demands and desires of existing customers who have been identified as 'valuable' to the Casino and 'coded' to us as Hosts.

But you also ask us to invent strategies that will:

1.   Attract and retain new valuable players,

2.   Maintain and grow existing players,

3.   Re-activate players that have disappeared or declined.

We all know that we need to do this, but we cannot proactively reach out and call 'missing customers' while we are also reacting to players in the noisy Casino. So, we need some quiet time in the office.

There must be guidelines on the amount of time spent 'in the office working the phone' versus 'working the Casino floor'. It's all about balance.

Sometimes, dear General Manager, you send a conflicting message to your PD team. On the one hand, you want us to grow the business by making proactive phone calls and sending appropriate texts, emails and letters. But, on the other hand, we have heard you complain that we are 'sitting in the office' and not out on the floor meeting guests.

By designing a set of goals that measure all these different efforts and results, you can create a framework that enables us to correctly spread our time and energies across this range of challenges.

Thank you!

How to Meet and Exceed Your Goals

Here is a generic approach that you can follow to build momentum and keep the numbers growing instead of stagnating.

PRIORITIZE! Take an honest look at your goals and decide how hard they are:

Which goals seem more like low-hanging fruit and can be achieved most readily? Set aside a couple of hours a week on these.

Which goals will take the most work to achieve? Decide to spend a lot of time on these each week. An hour a day, every day, before you go out to meet guests?

Get started now on the hardest goals! A 12-week Quarter may seem like a long time, but it will disappear in no time.

When you make a call, you are going to drive a trip within the next week or two (or longer if you call a guest that is not local and has to plan their trip). There are 12 weeks in the Quarter so making a call in the 9th week is the last chance that you have to make a difference to this quarter's results. In the last two weeks of the Quarter, you are actually making calls that will drive trips in the next Quarter! Do not leave everything to the last minute...

> "I watch my Hosts closely. My successful people work on their KPIs every day. They make time to call their guests and they constantly discuss their strategies with me. They don't blow hot and cold. I have one Host who leaves everything to the end of the Quarter and then it is too late."

PLAN! Come up with an approach to each goal. This is where each Host will bring their unique ideas based on their experience and personality.

Is a Goal to increase Theo from Active Players by 10% over last Quarter? Perhaps you decide (1) target the highest-ADT patrons who are off pace for their usual trip pattern, and (2) target the people who were new last Quarter and could probably play-up now they know the property.

Is a Goal to re-activate 5 valuable Inactive players who haven't played for six months? Maybe start by working the ones who live closest to the property? Maybe ask Direct Mail for the list of offers sent to Inactive guests and use that as the hook. Place a call and say "Hey, I'd hate for you to miss this Free play that you were sent. Let's get you in to this Event next week and you can play on the House".

If you are new to this approach, then ask your Manager and more experienced peers for some suggestions.

CLASSIFY! As we discussed earlier, you have to know which players fall into which classification. And this will change over time as they do, or don't, visit and play high. If your management team requires you to achieve goals, then you are going to need adequate reporting and preferably a Host CRM.

DISCIPLINE! Create a plan and stick to as best you can. Perhaps this is your plan when you first come on shift: (1) Make a list of 5 Inactive players to call right now. (2) Make a list of 10 Active players to call during the shift. (3) Carry this list around with you and make phone-calls between dealing with guests, or while you are standing around waiting for the Entertainer to show up. Be prepared and then you can maximize your time.

MEASURE! Understanding progress is key to keeping yourself on track. If what you're doing isn't working, wouldn't you rather know early on, so you have time to change tactics before the period ends?

Break your quarterly goal up into 12 weeks. If you have to re-activate 24 Inactive guests then you need $24/12 = 2$ guests per week, coming back and playing. If you need to grow Theo by 240,000 per quarter, then it needs to grow by $240,000/12 = 20,000$ per week.

Database might agree to pull a weekly or monthly list for you that shows who played and their Theo this quarter. If this is hard to get for yourself then give a specific example to the PD Manager of what would help the team and ask them to approach Database.

Some Host CRMs can tell you on a Daily basis whether you are on pace or whether an additional push might be necessary to achieve the goal for increasing Theo etc. With this knowledge, you can adjust call patterns, prospecting plans, or events bookings to bring the numbers back in line.

REFLECT! Whether a particular goal period was successful or not, you should take some time at the end of the Quarter, to think about what worked and what didn't,

This is the time when all the variables need to be assessed:

Was weather a factor? Then maybe do a snow day special that gives patrons a premium for coming in within 7 days of the crappy weather.

Did a high number of valuable guests just not play? Maybe a personalized handwritten letter with a special offer is the way to go.

Are you having trouble getting prospects coded? Perhaps it's time to rethink how you choose prospects…or it's time to talk to your team leader about how to qualify them for becoming coded players.

DON'T GIVE UP!!! Be honest with yourself about what you did and didn't do well. Improve your plans, your lists, and your approach. Talk to others on your team and to Management. Perhaps reach out to someone you know at a different, non-competitor, property and brainstorm with them about different approaches for different groups of players and goals.

Remember that there is rarely a single factor that dictates success or failure. Once you have a plan, it is daily persistence that works.

"Ambition is the path to success.
Persistence is the vehicle you arrive in."
Bill Bradley

Pace Reports

A pace report shows you where you stand so you can monitor their performance and adjust your tactics before it is too late.

To create a Pace report, we figure out three things:

(1) What is the percentage of the Goal? If your coded players have made 2,505 trips and the goal is 5,010 trips, then you are 2505/5010 = 50%.

(2) What is the percentage of the quarter? If we are in Q2 then there are 91 days from April 1st through June 30th. If yesterday was April 16th, the 16th day of Q2, then we are at 16/91 = 18% of the quarter.

(3) Finally, we compare the two percentages to determine if the you are Ahead, On Goal, or Behind. If you already have 50% of your trips and we are only at 18% of the quarter, then you are most definitely Ahead! Congratulations!

Ask your Manager for a regular Pace report from the Database team, from IT, or from your Host Software. A daily pace is available from some Host Software programs and that is invaluable because it helps you to keep momentum.

Build Strategic Momentum

Successful Hosts intuitively understand and care about momentum.

You cannot take random steps to grow your players and expect results. You have to be consistent and put in some effort each and every day to grow your book of business. Commit to making so many phone calls each day and commit to writing so many emails or letters each week. Decide to call every single person the week before their Birthday to see if you can get them in, and then commit to calling them on their Birthday as well.

Being consistent on a daily basis creates internal and external momentum.

Internally, you will see yourself as a disciplined and strategic player development professional who knows how to 'do the work'. This increased sense of self-worth will help you continue to learn and grow.

Externally, you will be creating momentum in the behavior of your players. If you randomly call a player, then they might come in within the next two weeks just because you placed your Resort Casino at the top of their mind. But if you systematically call, write, text and meet your players then they will become your loyal guests. And you will get to the point where they visit because you ask them to (!) and then you have matured from Casino Host to Player Development Executive.

Here are the steps:

(1) Decide on your personal strategy, your personal plan for growing your guest.

(2) Start now! Not next week but now.

(3) Keep going! A little bit each and every day!

You won't immediately feel the change because it takes time for your actions to have an effect but be persistent and execute your strategies on a daily basis.

> "Hosts must be pro-active! Don't wait for your guests to call you for a weekend getaway or to plan their birthday. Stay on top of it and your guests will surely be happy. Time block your day with making phone calls, email/text upkeep, and floor time. Give yourself a consistent daily plan to keep yourself not only busy but on top of your book. Having a CRM can help immensely when it comes to segmenting your time appropriately, so that you are using your time effectively."

Strategic Reasons To Call (RTC)

Once you commit yourself to regularly reaching out to all of your players, you quickly realize that you can only call so many times with the generic question '*How are you?*'.

You need good reasons to call; and these are literally called Reasons To Call (RTC) by sales reps who make outbound calls to customers and prospects. With a good reason to call, you will sound enthusiastic and you can find an angle that conveys to the guest that you genuinely thought about them. This is the why the 'Happy Birthday' call is so easy to make. You sound totally sincere when you give them Birthday wishes.

Here are some other examples of good Reasons To Call:

Did You Hear? When your Resort Casino announces a new amenity, such as a golf course, you can call your guests that are golfers and ask them *Did you hear about our new golf course?* The amenity does not have to be complete, in fact it is better if you can make three calls out of this one situation. *Did you hear we are building?* and *Did you hear that we open in three weeks, let's get you in* and *We are open!*

I Bet You Are Happy. You should follow the local sports teams and track which of your players are raving fans. When the team gets through to the next round, you can place the *I bet you are happy* call and listen to them talk all about the game.

Did You See? We talked earlier about the idea that you should be tracking the Direct Mail offers. You can call and say *Did you see your $100 in free play next month? I'd hate you to miss your offer in all your mail. Let me know if you can't find it?*

This is a great strategy if you have seasonal players. Let's say that Paul usually goes away in August and returns in April every year. In March, you can find out Paul's offers from the Direct Mail team and then call Paul in Florida. *Hi Paul! I am thinking it is nearly time for you to come back? I know your mail sometimes doesn't follow you to Florida and I want to make sure you have seen your free play for April?*

I Thought Of You. As you walk the Property, pay attention to the promotions, events and special offers. You can call and say *I thought of you this afternoon because we have a special Surf and Turf. Did you see it?* If there is a change in the slot mix in the High Limit room, or a commitment to always having a $20 blackjack table open, then you can call a whole list of people to say *I thought of you, did you notice the changes to the…*

What Did You Think? If there has been an upgrade to the cocktail bar with a really cool new layout and some stunning effects then wait a few weeks, pull a list of recent players, and call a whole list of people to ask *What do you think of the new cocktail bar? I'd love to get your opinion.*

How Are You? If you are doing a good job of tracking your regular players, then you will notice when someone has broken their pattern for visits. You can call with the *I have not seen you for a while. Is everything okay? Or have you been on a great vacation?*

Welcome Back. If you learn that someone is going away, or going into hospital, then you make a note to contact them on their return. *I hope you had a great vacation! Tell me about Hawaii!'* or 'Welcome home, I just wanted to wish you a speedy recovery.*

This is a starting point and you will come up with your own comfortable list of different types of Reasons To Call (RTC). You can also talk to your peers and ask others online via social media to see what ideas they have.

You should keep notes on that guest, and how well they responded, so you can take a different approach the next time and add variety to the on-going conversation.

Guest Preferences

In addition to your notes about previous contacts, you need to be aware of their preferences. If they don't answer the phone, then choose another method. Send them a text! Keep fishing around until they respond or, if you meet them in person, ask them their preference.

Communicate based on the patrons' preferences, not your own. If I'm your player and I tell you I'd rather you text me, then I am going to be annoyed if you insist on making a phone call.

Try different approaches until they respond, including varying the time of day, or day of week. You might be surprised at what works best for them! E.g. a text on a Saturday morning.

Strategic Telemarketing

Part of your job is to interact face to face with the people who are here playing, and part of your job is to reach out to the people who are not here. There is a big difference between engaging a person with your eyes and smile and placing an outbound call to someone who might not want to hear from your right now.

Do you find yourself lacking the confidence and skills to place an un-invited phone call?. You might avoid making the calls altogether, or you might start the call strongly and then ramble incoherently.

Making sales calls is particularly difficult. You are going to be cold-calling players to sell them on making a trip, staying in the hotel, attending an Event, and more.

> "When I hire, I look for competitive drive. If you have that competitive spirit, then you do everything it takes to win; to not only meet the goals but beat them. Even so, some people really struggle initially with getting around the guest's objections and stone-walling. 'I need to talk to my husband' or 'I am not sure if we can make it'. Hosts must never ever give up. And that drive comes from a competitive mindset."

You should go on-line and find videos, books, and more that will help you to refine your sales skills and get around the objections. Selling is about persistence, but it is also about technique.

You might also want to suggest to your Manager that they budget for onsite training for your team on how to place effective out-bound calls to 'close the deal' and get the player to commit to the next trip. Do the research yourself and make a couple of recommendations (so your Manager does not have to do the work.)

It is best to make this recommendation just before the start of the budgeting cycle which is probably July or August. You can ask the Manager or someone friendly in the Finance team to find out when. Once the budget is locked in and approved, there won't be any additional money available to pay for training.

Select a trainer who is prepared to do role play and listen in to some of your actual phone calls, so they transfer skills and do not just speak to the theory.

6 Tips for Telemarketing

In the meantime, here are some things to think about:

1. **Make a Plan.** Be clear in your mind about your Reason To Call, and the outcome you want to achieve. Are you calling to touch base, to get information, or to close their commitment to an Event? What are you going to say if they decline? How will you respond if they are irritated at the interruption?

2. **Be Ready For Voicemail.** Decide ahead of time whether you are going to hang up or leave a voicemail. If you are going to leave a voicemail, then plan what you are going to say so you are not recording any 'Ums'. Write this message down so you are ready to roll when you are dropped into voicemail.

3. **Rev Yourself Up!** You don't want to get into the phone with over-the-top crazy enthusiasm! But your voice and words had better convey some passion about what you are describing. Literally standing up is a good idea because your voice has more energy if you are not slumped in a chair. Plus, you will tend to walk about and be more animated.

4. **Visualize them!** Imagine them standing in front of you. What do they look like? How do they approach a conversation? What are their personality traits? The trick is to mentally climb down inside that phone and stand right in front of them!

5. **It's Not About You.** Put yourself in a mindset that begins and ends with the player's best interests at heart. If you can focus on how you are trying to help them, they will hear that tone in your voice and respond well. Even if they are not interested in your information, they will be grateful that you cared. For example, they may say, '*I am not interested in this concert but please keep me in mind next time.*'

6. **Grab Their Attention.** Don't start with a tentative '*Am I interrupting you?*' because they will think Yes! Use their name and quickly get to what you hope will interest them. Practice your opening line and hook them with something interesting. 'Mike, this is Sam, I have something really cool to tell you...'

7. **Make Them Feel Special.** Use their name, mention the names of their family and friends if you have those Notes, ask open questions and listen hard, and be sure to thank them for their time.

It is exhausting to make a lot of calls plus you will start to be bored with repeating your 'pitch' so be realistic about how many calls you can make in a row. Pace yourself and make 5 a day for 5 days instead of 25 calls on one day.

Stay hydrated (with water not caffeine), eat a light lunch, stretch, stand up to call, walk around the outside of the building at lunchtime, take the stairs for extra exercise, and breathe deeply before you call to focus yourself. All of these techniques will convey healthy energy in the quality of your voice.

And finally, practice, practice, practice. The drive to work is a great opportunity to talk out loud and imagine that you are making calls! Who cares what the other drivers think of your crazy antics.

Invest In Yourself

Throughout this chapter, we have encouraged you to invest time and effort into classifying your players, tracking your players, and proactively reaching out build and sustain the relationship. In addition, you should be investing time and effort in yourself.

The Strategic Host is not only making strategic decisions to achieve their immediate goals but also carving out time and energy to achieve their long-term personal goals.

Do you want to be the Best Possible Host? Invest time and effort to consistently meet and exceed your goals. This will position you well for job security, pay raises, and bonuses. You will come to know your coded players so well that this actually becomes easier and easier.

(Until a new General Manager arrives and insists on a crazy 25% growth in Theo over the same quarter next year! Then you have to start prospecting among the un-coded players and change your mix and your approach.)

Do you want to move into management? In addition to meeting your goals, you should focus on the mechanics of running a team and studying sales techniques so that you could put in place an amazing approach to driving revenue from your future team of Hosts. Learn about Host CRM software, dramatically improve your MS Excel skills, and learn about how databases, reporting tools, and business intelligence could help to classify players. Attend sales training. Read sales management books on how to set goals and bonus schemes that will drive the behavior that you will want from your team.

Do you want to become a Player Development Executive? Focus on how to expand into the personal network of your best players. Who are their friends that visit Vegas? Who are their family members that are self-made multi-millionaires and like to gamble? You also need to think more about psychology. Why do people gamble? What motivates them to fly across the country and play for a long weekend in a remote location? What do they crave that they cannot buy with money? What experiences can you create for them?

As a Strategic Host you look beyond what is facing you today and think about what you want to achieve in the future.

As a Strategic Host, you don't react to what is going on around you each day, you literally Seize the Day (Carpe Diem!) and execute to your long-term plans.

And as a Strategic Host, you don't just bounce from issue to issue. You have a thoughtful approach that enables you to analyze what is happening around you, and to learn ever deeper lessons about how people behave, what gamblers really want, and how to position yourself to win in every situation.

Finally, if you work for a Property that doesn't even understand what the role of a host is, and thinks you are an overpaid greeter, then either educate them on your value or move to a Resort Casino that understands the value of the position. Because you cannot grow without support and encouragement.

Self-Assessment

Before you read on, grab a pen and complete this self-assessment. Where are your areas for improvement?

Skill	Always	Most of the time	Rarely
I classify my players in my mind. I could tell you the different ways that I think about them.			
I classify my players in MS Excel or some kind of software			
I keep track of their trips and play on a regular basis, so I know exactly what is happening with them.			
I meet or exceed my KPIs / Goals			
I call everyone on their Birthday or just before the day			
I have my own list of Reasons To Call			
I know how my guests like to be contacted and at what time/day			
I invest extra time and effort in growing my skills because I know what I want to achieve.			
I believe I can grow at my current Property.			

What Is Your Work Ethic?

This morning, I was listening to Gary Vaynerchuk talk about the need for a strong work ethic, and that all successful people have, to quote Gary, 'worked their face off'.

I was thinking about that. I don't want to work my face off, if that means working 18 hours a day, every day. I want to have time away from work, I want to enjoy all aspects of my life, and I want to be healthy physically, emotionally, and socially.

But I'm not lazy. I do have a strong work ethic.

Each day, I **complete** whatever has to be truly done that day. This means that I have to be very clear about 'importance'. (If I tried to finish everything on my To-do list then I would never stop working; just like the washing up, those new To-dos pile up as quickly as I put the old ones away.) So, I am brutal about deciding what has to be done that day and I will work late into the night if necessary.

I do **everything** that I don't want to do. There are many things, large and small, that I don't want to do. Like a toddler! I don't want to! But I have learned to recognize that feeling, let myself be unhappy, and then buckle down and get them done. If I procrastinate and put them off, then they are living in the back of my mind and making me miserable. If I step up and get them finished, then they are gone. (I didn't expect so many positive aspects of Yoga. I think the regular practice of Yoga trains the mind to understand the emotion, and then move beyond it.)

I am **fearless**. Part of a strong work ethic is to be able to 'do what needs to be done' regardless of one's fear. Back in my 20's and 30's, I used to live with a lot of fear, and I made a mess of so many situations. But now I live by the rule 'Challenge your limits, don't limit your challenges'. If I fail at something, then it doesn't matter because certain people still love me. And, of course, if I make a mistake then I will say so, and own it, because integrity is key in business.

I am **disciplined**. Four months ago, I decided to start writing articles and books, and sharing much of what I have learned from working with some fabulous Player Development professionals over the years. I decided to write one article a week. I don't always "want to" but I have to because that is my commitment to myself.

Listen to motivation videos and podcasts at the start of your day to get you into the right frame of mind.

I am **organized**. I maintain three To-do lists. One is for my personal life, one is for Harvest Trends now, and one is for Harvest Trends future. Each morning, I review each list (and yes, these are hand-written on paper, using my Dad's Parker Pen and real ink. People are often amazed that I don't use a software tool but, because I knock these things out, they don't grow into long lists.) I pick 3 items to be completed today; that way, there is plenty of room for the other tasks that pop up during the day and must be knocked back. I think of incoming tasks/emails as if they were ping-pong balls, and I am an Ace table tennis player! I want to knock those little white balls back over the net as they arrive, and not have them all land on the floor around my desk.

I am constantly reading, listening and **learning**. To me, part of having a strong work ethic, is to work on myself as much as my 'job'. I multi-task this into my life. For example, I listen to motivational speeches while I am getting ready in the morning, or if I am working on a task that does not require much mental attention.

And I am always, always, always **thinking**. I will see an article on a completely different industry and I will be thinking about what it means to Player Development. So, yes, I am a little obsessed in that way!

I do work a lot of hours, but I don't work my face off and I don't expect to become a billionaire. What is your work ethic? What does as strong work ethic mean to you?

Chapter 7. T IS FOR THOUGHTFUL

Thoughtful means being going beyond kind, and actually taking the time to be considerate. Thoughtful means paying attention. And thoughtful means thinking about things.

Empathy not Sympathy

There is no way for a Player Development professional to build relationships with a diverse set of casino guests without consistently employing a lot of empathy.

What is Empathy? Empathy means you can understand how others feel.

The Empathetic Host is focused on really understanding the guest's situation, attitude, and behaviors. This is a thought process that is often instinctive but can be learned.

There are five key skills and they can all be improved with thoughtful practice:

1. What is the **body language** of the guest? What can you deduce from the way they walk, the way they gesture, and the way the stand in front of you?

2. What is the **facial expression** of the guest? What can you tell from the shape of their mouth, and the position of their eyebrows?

3. How do they **sound**? What is their tone, the speed of their speech, the volume of their voice?

4. What are they really **saying**? Behind their choice of words, what message are they really trying to send to you?

5. And finally, what can you learn by asking open-ended questions?

   An **open-ended** question, such as, 'Why are you so disappointed?', can lead to many answers. A **closed** question, such as 'Do you want a comp?', will only lead to one of two answers, Yes or No. Okay! It will always lead to Yes!

These skills create the ability to understand the other person and can be constantly improved upon, by continuing to sharpen our skills in interpreting body language, reading facial expressions, listening for tone, probing for underlying issues, and asking open-ended questions.

Empathy is the key to successfully developing meaningful relationships with your coded players. And, constantly improving your skills of insight, will lead to more Empathy in dealing with fellow Hosts, working across departments within the Casino, and probably to a promotion because Empathy is key to being a successful Manager.

If my guest is angry because they showed up for the Ham Giveaway Promotion and there is nothing left, then I can have complete **empathy** but not necessarily **sympathy**. After asking some open questions, I can realize that they left home too late and they are mad at themselves, but that they want to express themselves as frustrated at the Casino. With this empathy, I can decide on my approach. And without sympathy, without actually feeling sorry for them, I can still use my professional face and demeanor to handle the situation.

Sympathy means feeling compassion, sorrow, or pity.

If you think about it, having a Big Heart and being Sympathetic to your guests, could lead to your emotions clouding your judgement, let alone to you crossing the invisible line and befriending your players.

Empathy means you understand what they are feeling; and Sympathy means your own mood changes and responds to theirs.

I suggest that you constantly refine your ability to be Empathetic and double-check any impulse to be Sympathetic.

Not that it is bad to care but, as a professional, you are in the business of consistency and your emotional reaction (positive or negative!) may lead you to react differently to different people. And that always leads to trouble. So! Use all of your skills to understand but keep your heart in check, and act from your head. What we are discussing here, is Emotional Intelligence.

Emotional Intelligence

Emotional Intelligence is the capacity to be aware of, control, and express one's emotions, and to handle interpersonal relationships judiciously and empathetically.

Emotional intelligence allows you to 'read' your guests and know 'where they are coming from'. The intelligence to accurately recognize another person's emotions through their words, body language, and facial expressions.

> "A successful host can read people. Read their body language and decide their mood before talking to them. If they are in a bad mood, then ask about the kids or grand-kids because that will make them light up. If you don't know them, then talk about the weather because that is a neutral topic. If their body language says they are in a good mood, then talk to them about their wins".

You have found your way into a role that requires sales skills and customer service instincts, so you are probably naturally high in emotional intelligence. But it is still a good idea to read articles and books and learn more.

Your high emotional intelligence also enables you to respond appropriately with your own words, body language and facial control. You already know that your body language and facial expressions are really important in making people feel comfortable and welcome. As a Casino Host, you need an immaculate control of your body language, and use of Emotional Intelligence, so that you convey open friendliness to the most *#&@^ personalities.

Cultural Variations

There are tremendous cultural variations in everyone's behavior based on where and how they grew up, and where and how they live now, and that can completely throw off your Emotional Radar.

I am British, I've lived in the US for over 30 years, and go back to England twice a year to visit my elderly mother. As I interact with her friends, and with the shopkeepers, I realize every now and then that I have done something slightly inappropriate! I have a strong enough Emotional Radar to pick up on their reaction, but I don't know my mistake because I have forgotten so many details about how to interact in this culture.

This is one of the challenges for a Casino Host when they move cross-country into a different culture, or into a very different Property where the guests have different expectations.

You can practice now by paying detailed attention to all of the different personalities among your players and the subtle, or not so subtle, differences in how they interact. Learn to slightly adjust your approach in way that they don't consciously notice but it improves how they respond to you.

Thoughtful Respect

Many of your most valuable players are 60+ because at that age they have the time and the disposable income. These guests may be twice your age so how can you relate to them?

The emotionally intelligent approach is to show respectful interest and ask open questions. These guests will greatly appreciate your respect as you take the time to ask about their lives, to hear their stories (perhaps repeated over and over!) Did they serve the country? Then remember to thank them on Veterans Day.

Look at this lovely photo from Tom Hussey: You will start to realize that, in their minds, your guests are only 21.

Think Before You Speak

Always maintain confidentiality. It is easy to forget who is around when you are speaking with co-workers or even other guests. If you are going to be talking about specific player patterns or proprietary company information, always ensure you are in an area away from guests as well as employees who do not have access to the information you are sharing.

Never reveal things like ADT ranges or levels, customer losses, company policies and procedures, or sensitive information like room numbers or addresses.

When speaking with a customer directly, use generalizations or anecdotes to share pertinent information without going into specific unless you are talking about that guest's own play patterns. Even then, only use points or another metric which the customer can plainly see for himself to make your point.

Think about your Brand

You work in an industry where everyone talks to each other across casinos and everyone moves around. When you apply to a different casino, there will be informal phone calls made between friends and acquaintances to check you out. Phone calls that you will never find out about but that can make or break your career.

Protect your brand or you will shut yourself out of future job opportunities. Or worse, you may end up in jail!

You don't want to be the Host that is discussed as '*Did you hear about so and so? What were they thinking?*' Well, you weren't thinking straight and that is how you got into trouble.

I am going to share some of the problems, and even outright scams, that have damaged people's careers and even lives. Why? Because I don't want you to think that you can get away with any of these behaviors. You are being watched and the Casino has all kinds of policies and techniques in place to monitor your behavior.

I know that you have high integrity and would never participate in any of these nefarious activities, but I want you to be aware, so you can spot trouble brewing.

Think About Consequences

If you are suspicious, tell your manager. If you do not say anything and the situation blows up, you could get dragged into the investigation by the Gaming Commission and that could affect your Gaming License. Without the ability to get a License, you are finished.

Please be alert to the following:

1. **Affairs with Players**. This is so commonplace. The job requires a friendly relationship at all hours and people do cross over the line into an affair. Is this you? **Do not fool yourself for one minute that no-one knows.** For one, the other Hosts are all really good at picking up on the body language and chemistry between you and the player. And the Casino is monitoring the incoming and outgoing calls on your work phone and checking for frequent, or particularly long, interactions.

   Why does the Casino care? Because if you are having an affair with a player then you are at risk of committing fraud because of your favoritism, and you are at risk of being blackmailed into ignoring crimes such as laundering money.

2. **Affairs with Managers**. This is more common that you might expect. Casino Executives move around every two to three years and they often do not relocate their families because of the upheaval. This leaves the Casino Executive with way too much alone time. Again, do not fool yourself that no-one knows. Everyone knows, and you are a laughing stock.

   I recall sitting at a table in a restaurant on property and the server did not have enough glasses of water. "*Oh, that doesn't matter*", said the GM, "*I will drink out of hers*" and he picked up the glass of an Executive Host. The gossip had spread around the casino staff before we even reached the desert course.

3. **Rigged Drawings**. It can be too easy to rig the outcome of a Drawing to benefit an accomplice. 'Mary' wins the prize, sells it, and shares the proceeds with the casino employee. You might find yourself pressured by a manager to rig the drawing to placate an unhappy guest. There was a case in Vegas where a high roller received a Mercedes Benz SUV to placate him for heavy losses during Chinese New Year. If this happens you immediately tell the other person that you refuse to participate.

Whenever you are involved in a Drawing, go out of your way to ensure it appears above board because everyone is watching. You should also be ready to explain to an investigator how you designed the process to be sure that no-one could cheat.

4. **Free Play scams.** There was a high profile case of collusion between a VP Player Development, a beverage server and a guest. The server would collect player reward ID and PIN numbers while taking drink orders. The VP would make bogus reward cards loaded with free slot play credits. The customer would gamble with the free play and then share any winnings. There are all kinds of variations on this theme. People get caught because the Audit team discovers a pattern in the numbers, or someone turns them in.

5. **Comp scams.** The scam is that the Host issues a comp to an accomplice, friend (or lover!) by charging the comp balance of a different player. This scam is usually for smaller dollar amounts.

6. **Points scams.** A casino employee looks for accounts with a high point balance, but the guest rarely comes in or hasn't played for months. The employee issues a new card for that Account and gives it to an accomplice to burn the points. These people get caught because the Audit department sees the pattern in the numbers and the PIN resets.

7. **Selling Merchandise.** Casino Hosts have been caught and arrested for taking promotional items and selling them off-property.

8. **Shills.** Someone is recruited to open a credit line, sit next to an actual player and gamble with borrowed chips. The real gambler is basically about able to play without a paper trail.

9. **Laundering and Theft.** If you have the slightest suspicion that your player is laundering money or playing with another person's money, then notify your manager. A Casino Host

went to jail because the guest said, "I need to win this money back because it isn't mine, I am playing with my investors' money." The Host did not take any action and so he was dragged into the court case when the investors finally found out and the money was gone.

10. **Adjusting Ratings.** These days, there should be systems and procedures in place to prevent this, but the concept is that the Host adjusts the Manual ratings to help them to meet their KPIs or to bump up the offers for an accomplice.

11. **Bribes.** Casino Hosts have been caught accepting cash bribes from guests to receive better hotel rooms, larger comps, the best tickets to a show, or to be invited back stage to meet an entertainer. A Host has so many benefits that they can direct to a guest. This is why you should avoid accepting any kind of **gift,** and definitely not cash, because of the risk of someone questioning your integrity. Talk to your manager and find out the policy on gifts.

12. **Services in Kind.** Many VIPs have businesses and services off-property that they can offer the Casino Host. A free limo for your wedding. A free meal at their restaurant for you and your partner. A lakeside cottage that is free for you to use over the weekend because the guest is never there.

    You should avoid any of these kinds of offers to prevent yourself being compromised or even suspected of complicit behavior. If you have a genuine opportunity to develop the player, then discuss the situation ahead of time with your manager. For example, a guest invites you to go deep sea fishing with his friends who usually play at another casino and you want to build a relationship and pull them in.

Bear in mind that these scenarios often start for very low dollar amounts and the Host may not intend to carry on. But once someone has stepped over the line, they can be blackmailed into getting in deeper. If you do make a mistake in judgement then it is best to tell your manager now and face the smaller consequences.

You might think that no-one is looking but every General Manager is aware of these scams and more, and every Casino has people dedicated to looking for patterns of behavior and patterns in the data that will eventually show up the fraud.

If you have your suspicions about someone else, then you have three choices:

1. You could approach them directly and let them know that you are aware and that you are worried about them; this may scare them into stopping but it could also be very awkward between you.

2. You could tell your manager and emphasize that you don't want the other person to know that this came from you.

3. And if you are in a truly precarious position, such as your direct manager being implicated, then you might consider delivering an anonymous tip-off to the Gaming Commission via a physical letter.

Be a Defensive Host

We have talked about some pretty shady practices that you won't see every day, but you will see in the course of your Casino career. Let's shift gears and wrap up with the reality that you will face every single day.

"As a rule, the relationships you build with your players will become second nature after a time. **They may begin to feel like your actual friendships**. You'll learn which of your players are interested in what sort of events at your casino. You'll figure out which ones want more comps than their play warrants (manage them carefully!) and which ones would rather just be left alone to play. It won't take you long to remember what brand of smokes your best players prefer, and which restaurants each of your better players frequent. Who golfs, who owns his own business, who takes care of their grandchildren on weekends, who gets all worked up if you don't return their call within a couple of hours…you get the idea. "

Yes, they may begin to feel like your actual friendships. Especially as you are spending the majority of each day in the Casino and, to be a VIP player, they are probably there all the time as well!

Are you a friend? Of course not. Don't get too friendly or you can easily cross a line that leads to no end of trouble for you.

"Players feel a need to give back to those who give to them. This brings up the question: How close should your hosts get with players? I've seen this happen over and over again and there is not any other way to say it then this: hosts need to stay professional and not mix business with personal relationships. If you keep the relationship in a business manner, players respect the host and maintain a longer relationship with the casino."

A General Manager shared a story with me regarding a Host who crossed a line and ended up in trouble. It involved a young Host becoming 'too friendly' with some guests and going off-premise to join them for food and drinks. Because, of course, the Host could not drink on property. An F&B Manager was aware of this, and even ended up joining the group off-property! The story did not end well. The Host, a woman, went to HR and the Police with an accusation and everyone was dragged into What Really Happened?

In my own professional life, I have found myself in a bad situation where it was all about 'My Word against Their Word' but it was a fellow employee and not a customer. If you are the employee and 'they' are the customer, then you are immediately less likely to be believed.

And even if you are believed, there is still the terrible PR issue of the customer's complaint. The Casino must take responsibility for your actions, or perceived actions, and the Casino must clean up the mess. So, you are going to be in big trouble.

Let's go back to this story. Both the Host and the Manager should have thought a little more deeply about why they cannot drink on their own Property. It is not to be mean. It is because alcohol removes inhibitions and even if the employee can hold their drink, it doesn't mean that the customer can.

You drive defensively, watching out the other idiots who may run a light, not give a turn signal, or text and drive. As a Casino Host, you must work and live defensively, watching out for customers or fellow employees who might cross a line and drag you with them.

- How might it look if you are drinking off-property with a VIP customer? Don't do it.

- How might it look if you are up alone in the Penthouse with a group of guests drinking? Take someone with you!

- How might it look if your top player wins the best prize after you drew the ticket? Have someone else pull the tickets.

Here's the brutal reality. It doesn't matter what you are doing, it matters how it could be interpreted.

On property, you have the added protection of cameras so if a customer, or employee, accuses you of impropriety then Surveillance might be able to pull the tapes. Off-property, you don't that extra layer of protection.

And what about off-hours? Does the Casino own your entire life and so you cannot go bar-hopping or dancing? Well, for one, it probably depends where you live and how likely you are to run into your Coded Players!

The point is that you must Host defensively. Tell your Manager as soon as there is any reason to do so. Just so they are not taken off-guard and, perhaps, they can re-code the guest. I remember being told "I cannot tell my Manager because this high value player is a married woman". Well, don't be having an affair with a married woman, let alone the best slot player!

And as for friends… We all have friends, and we might have friends that play in the Casino. But if your fellow Host meets a bunch of party animals in the Casino and follows them off-site to hang out with them… then those are not their friends! The motive was not friendship but a good time, and parties can go sour.

If you **See something, Say something!** First to the person themselves and then, if necessary, to management. It may be embarrassing or difficult to speak to someone about their behavior, or a rumor of their behavior, but it will be much worse when you get pulled into HR, or the Gaming Authority, to explain what you knew and when.

> "Many hosts with whom I've worked have some players with whom they are close on a more personal level. While this is not necessarily a bad thing, it can go too far. Sharing things of a very personal nature is potentially problematic, as it changes the dynamic of your relationship.
>
> Spending time with a player outside the casino's walls is sometimes a part of the job, though there are instances where a host can find himself "owing" a guest for the experiences shared elsewhere.
>
> Instead of having the patron see you as their personal casino "concierge," they may begin to see you as a friend, and they'll expect your relationship to feel like an ordinary friendship, even though there are some boundaries you might soon find yourself banging your head against (or breaking)."

Ask the other hosts on your team (particularly those who are more experienced) how they handle certain situations and take the best practices from among them to make your own. When you talk to experienced Player Development professionals, they will tell your that integrity, their brand, their reputation, is priceless.

Self-Assessment

Before you read on, grab a pen and complete this self-assessment. Where are your areas for improvement?

Skill	Always	Most of the time	Rarely
I study the body language of a guest before I approach them.			
I decide on my opening line before I greet them.			
I read articles and books about different personality types.			
I know my Myers Briggs classification			
I notice how people from different backgrounds interact differently with me.			
I make sure that I interact with the older guests in a respectful manner and ask questions.			
I am conscious of the need to behave in an above-board way that could not be mis-interpreted.			
My manager would say that I am 100% honest and trustworthy.			

6 Tasks You Shouldn't Find on a Casino Host Job Description

Dear General Manager,

Have you ever seen a host running around the casino floor on a Saturday evening? He's heading to the pit to help break the news that this roulette player isn't getting a comp for the buffet tonight. He took a call from one of his players as he was leaving the tables, and now he's running for the hotel desk to greet a guest who's just checking in. He grabs the mic on the way and makes a jackpot announcement, since a slot attendant held out a note to him as he cruised by. His radio crackles, and he's off to the steakhouse to push back a reservation before he heads to the entertainment stage to do a promotional announcement.

Can you see him? Walking as quickly as possible without actually running, while dodging guests, trash cans, structural features, and cocktail servers. He's hoping to make it to his destination in one piece, knowing that it's just the next stop in what's going to be a long night. All too often voice mails go unchecked, players' questions go unanswered, reservations are un-cancelled, comps are left unwritten, and hosts are unfulfilled. It's sad to think that this happens in one of the most rewarding jobs a people person can find.

Here's how you can prevent all this from happening. Don't ask the host team to do things that run counter to their main objective. They are employed to do one thing: get your best players to spend as much of their gaming wallet with your property as possible.

Here are 6 Tasks that a Host should not be doing unless you have a very small property.!

Not doing overhead announcements. For anything. Really. This is an easy responsibility to leave with your players club and/or promotions team. Consider hiring a personality to record "standard" announcements and set them to run at particular times so your staff can concentrate on taking care of your players.

Not handling Registration. For anything. Really. No tournaments, no hotel check-ins, no VIP event tables, period. Hosts should be walking through the event talking with people, not stuck in one place doing administrative tasks unrelated to driving visitation.

Not handling all operational complaints. Part of a host's job is to smooth the ruffled feathers of an angry high-roller. It's not necessarily the host's job, however, to come to the steakhouse every time a guest says his meal hasn't met his expectations. It is of vital importance that F&B and PD come to an understanding about which players (and which situations) should be handled by a host and when the room's staff should be trained and empowered handle things themselves.

Not running promotions. I know. The hosts are charismatic, and the crowd loves them and blah, blah, blah. But the host should be working that crowd and finally meeting that elusive new player he's missed the last 3 visits, not stuck at the Promotions Desk swiping player cards or drawing the winner's name.

Not poring over reports to figure out who to call. Your host team will be more effective if they don't have to do the database mining themselves. Give them specific information, on a daily basis, that pinpoints which guests to call, which reservations to make, and which activities to complete.

Not making calls to players whose ADT is never likely to reach a level for hosting. You know which players I mean, right? The squeaky wheels who end up on a host's voicemail because they couldn't get a comp last time they were there, and a coffee shop server suggested the host could help them. The guest who hasn't been to your property in more than a year and wonders why he doesn't have coupons this month. These are not the players your host team should be spending their valuable time on. Again, front-line employees, including those in the call center, need to be trained and empowered to handle service recovery themselves, so they only escalate to the host-on-duty for the exceptional players.

Imagine if you had 600 players coded to you, and your number one objective was to get your best players to spend as much of their gaming wallet with your property as possible. How would you want to spend your time? Not taking care of administration and minor service recovery.

Please work with your Player Development and Operations teams to re-assign these six responsibilities to other front-line employees. Then challenge use to exceed our goals with all that extra time and some new tools! Thank you, General Manager,!

Chapter 8. YOUR NEXT CAREER MOVE?

"It's not about the cards you're dealt, but how you play the hand."
Randy Pausch

The fact that you are reading this book suggests that you are an ambitious person with a drive to learn and to grow. Right now, you may be focused on becoming the very best Casino Host or Executive Host, but you should also be thinking about your next career move and planning ahead.

The good news is that the gaming industry presents so many opportunities for your future career. You can focus on your sales skills and become a Player Development Executive, or move into management, or move sideways into Marketing or Operations. There is no reason why you cannot plot a path to General Manager if that is your dream. You should look at people's profiles in Linked In and see the route that they took to reach your target.

Unlike most industries, there are no certification requirements or strict rules about what it takes to move from one area of the Resort Casino to another. So, the gaming industry is your oyster provided you do the hard work to grow your experience, hone your skills, build your brand and your network, and be ready to seize the opportunity.

In this Chapter, we are going to explore how you can do the planning and preparation for when you meet your opportunity!

'Good fortune is what happens when opportunity meets with planning.' Thomas Edison

---

The best way to decide what you want to aim for next, is to pay attention to everyone around you, and see what catches your interest. Don't limit yourself to *'what could I do right now?'*, look at all of the different roles across the Resort Casino and ask yourself *'What do I want to do in the future? What looks interesting? Who has the cool job?'*

You may have to take a couple of steps to get to your goal, but you can. No-one was born a VP or a General Manager. They might have started out as a Dealer or a Security Manager.

How to Start

Once you have decided on your goal, you can create your personal plan to get there. Here are some steps to take, regardless of what you choose.

1. Go online and search for three job descriptions for that position.

2. Look through the job descriptions and see what they have in common.

3. Open up your own resume and re-write it for when you apply for the job. Literally copy and paste from the job description into your resume. For example:

   Proven ability to resolve guest disputes in an effort to restore confidence in the service we provide

   Work collectively with all departments involved in planning and executing player events both on-site and off-site.

   Must be proficient in developing annual budgets as well as quarterly goals with a proven track record of controlling labor costs and expenses.

4. Be candid with yourself. Where are the gaps between your current experience and the requirements in these job descriptions?

5. And now you just figure out how to fill the gaps!

People are hired, and promoted, into a job for which they appear to be ready. We do not hire or promote on a leap of faith. We do not say, "Oh let's hire this person and see if they can figure out how to do that new job". We hire the candidate because they already seem to be a 'fit'.

If you want to become a Player Development Executive, then you need to be building fierce personal loyalty from the best players and networking like crazy.

If you want to be promoted to Management then you need to already behave, dress, and speak like a Manager. It falls on your shoulders to transform yourself.

> "To get promoted a Host has to be consistent, organized, eager to learn, etc. but I think an important psychological change is when you first think of the operation from the business' perspective instead of the guests. Hosts tend to favor their players and that is what you want from a host but sometimes it is hard to make them understand it from the business' perspective. It doesn't mean you don't consider the players, but there is a shift that typically needs to be made. Managing employees, budgets, and property goals are fundamentally different than managing players."

Create a Personal Plan

You should create a personal plan to fill the gaps. There is always a way to fill the gaps but they all require initiative on your part. You are going to have to volunteer to take on additional roles without any extra pay, any overtime, or any kind of short-term benefit.

Here are three examples to get you started. First, we show the requirement from the job description and then we discuss how you could close that particular gap.

Proven ability to resolve guest disputes in an effort to restore confidence in the service we provide?

Who do you see as a role model for service recovery? Talk to them and ask about their approach.

Build close relationships with Guest Services, the Players Club Representatives, and the Pit Bosses. Ask them about the different issues that they have seen in their careers and how they approach unhappy guests.

Read articles and books about empathy, emotional intelligence, and influencing skills.

Volunteer to be the Host on Duty on the busiest shifts so you get the widest exposure to all of the different scenarios that can arise.

Aim to win any kind of monthly or annual recognition for guest service at your Property.

Work collectively with all departments involved in planning and executing player events both on-site and off-site.

There are always opportunities to help with Events! Review the earlier Chapter on Event Planning to see which areas you are unfamiliar with, and then volunteer to help, so you understand the entire process. Introduce improvements if you can. Volunteer to team up with someone from Marketing to streamline the process.

Search online for ideas for VIP Events and create your own events for your coded guests. Start small! But go through the entire process including a pro-forma to take to your boss.

Must be proficient in developing annual budgets as well as quarterly goals with a proven track record of controlling labor costs and expenses.

Go and take some management courses if that is your direction! Find someone in your network who has a business and ask them to take you through a budget. Volunteer to be on a management committee for your Church or some local organization and immerse yourself in their budgeting process.

Learn all about using MS Excel to create models and using PowerPoint to communicate ideas. Pay attention in team meetings whenever your manager talks about metrics and expenses. Read my other book, *Casino Host Goals*, to learn all about KPIs. And make sure you hit all of your KPIs every time!

These examples should get you started. If you get stuck, then use Linked In to find people from across the country who are in your dream job. Look at their backgrounds and find some people that made your move, give them a call and ask for help with ideas! How did they do it?

He who would accomplish little must sacrifice little; he who would achieve much must sacrifice much; he who would attain highly must sacrifice greatly.
— James Allen

In the short-term, you have to invest time, money, effort, and show initiative, but it will get you to where you want to be. Successful people set a goal, create a plan, commit themselves, and do whatever it takes to make it happen.

Build Your Local Network

Even in this digital world, it is still a case of **who** you know and not what you know.

Build your internal fan base. When an opening comes up, you want people to recommend you on their own initiative. Or who will say "Yes, that makes a lot of sense" when they hear your name being considered.

Without being a brown-nose, slowly cultivate a good working relationship with the Director of Marketing, Pit Bosses, Front Desk supervisor, Players Club Manager, and more. Find out who would be involved in making the decision.

> "I have seen people work hard at impressing the GM when the decision to replace me would not be addressed by the GM. There would be an interview committee made up of the Director of Marketing etc. and that is who they should focus on."

The simplest way to make a good impression on someone is to thank them and their team whenever it is deserved.

Drop an email to thank F&B for the buffet at the VIP party, compliment the Director of Marketing on a popular promotion, and pass on any complements that you hear from your guests, such as "I just want to let you know that one of my guests was raving about the quality of the seafood buffet".

Build Your National Network

You must also network across the industry because you might have to move to a different Property to achieve your goal. If you look on Linked In, you can see how people moved between Properties and Markets in order to get a promotion or to change direction in their career.

There are four reasons for this:

1. If your desire is to be Player Development Executive then you are going to have to move properties, and move between different kinds of markets, in order to grow a personal portfolio of players who will follow you wherever you go.

2. There are limited openings at your Resort Casino. If you are open to making a move there are thousands of casinos that you could apply to.

3. Your current management team believe they know you well, and they believe they know what you would bring to a new position. This works in your favor if you have really made your mark; but it is more likely to work against you because the Executives will 'want to bring in some new blood and some new ideas'. When you apply somewhere else, you become the 'new blood'.

4. If you want to move into management, it is hard to become the manager of your former peers. There may be some lingering resentment over your promotion, and it can be hard for you to gain authority over your former peers. Executives know this and so they won't want to create that situation. The

exception to this rule is if you have already established yourself as the leader of the team.

The Internet has made it possible for you to establish a network across the industry. As of now, the platform of choice is Linked In. For free, you can slowly build up a network of gaming professionals, and you can slowly build your presence and brand. Yes, I am deliberately saying slowly. It will quickly become apparent if you are desperately commenting on, liking, and sharing everything that is posted by the VPs and GMs. Pace yourself.

When you meet other gaming professionals, treat them like a valuable player and stay in touch, including with people that leave your property and go elsewhere. Develop and maintain relationships even if the person is, say, a Director of Slots and that is not your direction. This person might still be able to put in a good word for you at a future Property. And they might become a GM! Vendors are another good connection to have. Stay in touch with those sales reps because they hear about opportunities and can suggest your name. Yes, it happens.

With all this said, there is a danger in hopping between properties:

"I look for resumes which show an employee has moved up within their organization. It doesn't have to be a big promotion, but I like to see they've had some movement within at least one of their organizations. That means the people who have observed their work the most felt they excelled enough to promote. **I think it is a red flag if a person has only received promotions from moving properties.** It makes me wonder what they are saying about their previous job is true or they just know what to say to get through an interview."

Stand Out

First and foremost, be exceptional at everything you do.

The more work that you do to prepare yourself,
the more you will stand out

Your number one skill is the ability to sell. You have to demonstrate the ability to consistently sell the Property, the amenities, the concerts, and the events.

But, remember, the measure of your results is in the numbers. It doesn't matter if your guests love you, if you are not increasing Theo by 5% over last year, as requested. It doesn't matter if you are increasing Theo, if you are over-investing in your guests and arranging fancy VIP events that lose money.

> "I believe the best way to get the attention of management is to understand the budget, profitability and guest service and the dance that is required to do all three well. If your company doesn't require a proforma before approving a party, dinner, outing, etc. learn to do one anyway. If it's not going to make money for the organization, it's a bad idea."

And it doesn't matter how great your numbers are, if you are a pain in the neck. Follow the policies and procedures. Complete your assignments on time. Follow through on every detail for your guests and don't throw other departments under the bus in order to save your face.

> "There are Hosts that are super-great with the players, but they don't pay attention to the operational side. And there are Hosts that are okay-great with the players, but they also follow through, and they understand the reinvestment, and the strategies. These are the Hosts that will be promoted into management."

Share The Feedback

Think for a moment about the things you hear over and over again in conversations with your players. These are common themes, and it's likely that your players have discussed their feelings about your program with one another as well.

Are they getting more free play from your competitors? Since there's not much you can do about that, remind them that you provide them extra "value" for their visits by making it easier for them to make room or dinner reservations.

Do they tell you that they don't like your promotions? Get specifics and pass them along to the pertinent associates in your marketing department in order to provide those folks the direction they need to make those promotions more appealing. Share what you learn in order to keep your casino ahead of the curve.

Play well with others

> "I think the main reasons that Hosts fail are ego and lack of courtesy and/or teamwork. There is a thin line between ego and confident. Exude confidence when talking to your guests but humble enough to do the small things and not take things personally when working in a team."

Be a positive role model. Be a team-builder across the entire Property and bring people together. As a Casino Host, you work with every single department, so you are in a unique position to have a positive impact across the Property.

(You can also use this breadth of contact to learn everything, and I mean everything, about how the entire Resort Casino works. Learn the vocabulary used in Finance and Accounting, understand the challenges of the supply chain behind Food and Beverage, and talk to Slots about floor optimization. Read books, ask questions, and be a sponge. Ask the managers in other departments what they expect from the Player Development team and reflect on how your role can assist theirs. This free education in gaming, will enable you to better navigate the Property on behalf of your guests, and it will give you the grounding for a future career at any level of management.)

Show Initiative

Volunteer to work on projects and pick areas that will bring new skills and fill the gaps in your resume. Volunteer to work on a team that will make a vendor selection and learn all about defining business needs and evaluating solutions. Volunteer to interview new hosts and be their 'buddy' as they learn the ropes. Volunteer for the task force created by the GM to make recommendations on how to attract younger players.

> "Accept change as fast as you can. Be an early adopter. Don't resist or complain. Be constructive."

Ask your manager for opportunities:

> "It is important for managers to give people an opportunity to show what they can do. Each year, each of my Hosts get their own party to plan. I give them a budget and a few criteria for who to invite. They have to create pro-forma beforehand and post-forma afterwards. I watch them plan their party and I see how much help they need from me, and how they go about it."

Be Creative

We have talked elsewhere about being creative with your VIP parties and hosted events. But, as you learn more (and especially as you become more Organized from Chapter 4!) you can make suggestions to your manager. For example, are the Direct Mail offers all mailed at the same time? This means your valuable 500+ ADT guests are competing with thousands of 50+ ADT guests who are all calling in to book a room. You might suggest that offers to VIP guests are mailed one day earlier; two days earlier if the offer is going to Canada!

Always make your suggestions to your manager in a 1:1 situation so they can give you candid feedback. After all, you may have overlooked an important detail. Make your suggestion humbly so that the Manager doesn't suspect that you think they are an idiot.

And never make more work for your boss! If you are presenting an idea, then you should also be volunteering to put in the effort to make it happen. You don't say 'Here's a better way to organize concerts'. You do say 'I have an idea about events that I would like your feedback on. If you like what we come up with, then I'd be happy to work with the team on implementing this'.

When your ideas are implemented, then always try to measure them so that the result can go on your resume. Instead of "Invented new VIP events", your resume should say "Invented new VIP events that were 25% more profitable".

By the way, keep track of your KPIs so those numbers can go on your resume as well: "Managed a book of business and grew this by 6%+ each and every year for three years."

> "What Hosts can control is their performance and willingness to learn. During your tenure, keep in mind that each quarterly performance log, personally created promotion, and any other processes created by you, the host, for the benefit of the company, can be used as leverage for either your job promotion meeting or interview for another company. It's important to consistently perform above KPI's so that when the rare opportunity does present itself, you can confidently assert yourself as the prime candidate for promotion."

Be Patient

Be patient; don't over promote yourself, or come off as arrogant, and don't get known as 'the know it all'. There is a fine line between making suggestions and being perceived as critical of management or moving into the realms of fantasy.

Patiently play the long game. Be nice to everyone, yes everyone, because this the gaming industry is still relatively small, and people move around all the time. The person that you cut off because they cannot help you today, may become the GM who decides not to hire you in five years.

Listen patiently. You have two ears and one mouth, so you can listen twice as much as you speak. Treat everyone with respect and apply empathy to your fellow employees. Basically, give everyone that same 'PD Treatment'!

Patiently and persistently build up all of your different skills and experiences. Watch your role models in the Resort Casino and copy them. Why do they succeed? Figure it out and adopt their techniques into your style. Do you see Casino Hosts that fail? Why? What can you learn from them?

And don't become impatient and apply for that next position until you are 100% ready. You have a plan so execute it and don't try to jump ahead when you still have gaps in your resume. But, if you are ready, then push forward and carve your path like the person in the following Case Study.

"My Story"

"I started my gaming career at 18 years old as a player's club representative.

At that time hosts were the players club supervisors. **They didn't host a specific book and mainly served as the go to people for all issues**. I always wanted to become a supervisor and at that time thought that's why I wanted to be a host.

After a few years, Player Development was born and made into a separate department from the players club. They only had one director and 2 executive hosts. The remaining hosts were demoted and stayed with the players club.

Throughout this time, I got to work closely with the two executive hosts and director and assisted in any way I could so that I can learn more about the hosting world. **I thought at that time that hosting meant providing great guest service and issuing comps to fix problems.**

I tried for almost 9 years to become a host at the first casino I worked for and although I worked extremely hard, gave 120% every day that I worked, offered my loyalty and received nothing in return I learned the hard way that if I was going to be a host I had to leave them and venture off to gain the experience I needed to move up.

I left them for their competitor and was finally given the opportunity to become a casino host. In the beginning the management we had wasn't effective. Yes, I was a host and I had a book of 400 players, **but my job was more about being a problem solver.** We were the ones that every department went to when issues would arise with any guest not just those who were hosted. We were trained to wear different hats every day and dealt with case by case basis.

About a year after I started we finally hired an effective leader who taught me what a host should be. **That is when I learned that my main goal was to ensure I created positive experiences and relationships to increase revenue.**

I learned that player development meant finding those players who had the potential to play big and develop them into the highest VIP level possible.

Towards the end of my 4 years as a casino host, they tried to implement inexpensive trainings to teach us better sales techniques however without spending the money to give us the tools and resources we needed it was difficult to learn the right skills to truly be a sales host. This only made me hungrier to learn more about sales hosting than ever before.

When advancing was not an option I turned to LinkedIn and found a position as a Senior Executive Host with a larger organization.

Working for a corporation that is not afraid to invest in their employees for maximum return has been the best decision I ever made. Here I have the tools and resources I need to be successful in my position. **I have learned sales techniques and telemarketing skills that are proven to help me succeed in maximizing my guestbook revenue.**

The fire now burns even thicker working for a corporation that has given me so much in such little time that I've worked for. "

I asked for permission to include this real life story because it is a wonderful example of someone paying attention to what is happening, and not happening, in their career. This person realized what their passion was and then fought relentlessly to find the role that would let them grow and express themselves. Thank you for sharing!

Self-Assessment

Before you read on, grab a pen and complete this self-assessment. Where are your areas for improvement?

Skill	Yes	Could do Better	No
I know my next career move.			
I have found the job description and I am working on my plan to plug the gaps			
I watch other people as role models for good, and bad, behavior.			
I network across the Casino at all levels.			
I network across the Industry.			
I stay in touch with everyone that I meet.			
I invest time and money in my personal development.			
I watch for opportunities to volunteer and learn.			

Chapter 9. IN CONCLUSION

I am truly grateful to all of the people who contributed their time to the creation of this book, so we could all learn from their shared wisdom.

There were four questions:

1. What are the qualities in a successful host?
2. Why do people fail?
3. What is the #1 characteristic in a new hire?
4. How does a Host get promoted to management?

We've covered everything in the book so far but let's boil everything down into a short list:

<u>What are the qualities in a successful host?</u>

- Passion! Energized by interacting with people
- Natural ability to deal with people
- Ability to sell
- Confidence
- Follow through

<u>Why do people fail?</u>

- Don't follow through
- Don't try hard enough
- Give up too soon
- Ego. Greed. Lack of ethics.

The managers placed a lot of emphasis on the need for the PD professional to be detail oriented and follow through for the guest on an adjustment, a refund, a reservation or whatever.

I assume the managers placed an emphasis on this because they have to get involved when a customer is frustrated and unhappy. You may take the attitude that you don't make many mistakes but remember that your manager is dealing with the entire team 'not making many mistakes'. It counts for a lot if you never ever create any work for your manager.

What is the #1 characteristic in a new hire?

- Passion
- Confidence
- Drive – competitive spirit

How does a Host get promoted to management?

- Attention to detail
- Consistently follow all operational procedures
- Understand reinvestment
- Be able to sell and to coach others how to sell

I was pleasantly surprised by the consistency of the answers from Hosts, Executive Hosts, Player Development Executives, Managers, and VPs. Everyone gave similar answers.

I am a visual person and I enjoy statistics, so this pie-chart works for me to summarize everything that has been said in this book.

In equal parts, you need to love people, you have to be good as sales, you must think strategically even when deciding to issue a lowly comp, and you have to have a 100% commitment to following through.

So, let's go back to the beginning!

H – Happy to Help

O – Organized

S – Strategic

T – Thoughtful

The successful Host is always **Happy to Help**.

You realize that your #1 priority is to build a loyal relationship by consistently being there for your guests, but you also know that you must balance their demands with the overall profitability and strategies of the casino. You have honed your strategies for making a No sound like a Yes and you focus on educating your guest on how to get what they want.

The successful Host is **Organized.**

You are constantly finding new ways to be more efficient and more effective. You realize that an organized person is essentially a lazy person and does not want to do anything twice! Because you are organized, you always follow through, and you don't run around the Property looking like a maniac. You leave the building at the end of your shift with a sense of accomplishment and not with deep stress at the length of your task list.

The successful Host is **Strategic**.

You classify your players and you have your own strategies for maintaining, developing or retaining the different groups of players. You understand your goals, and you have plans in place to meet and exceed those KPIs. You don't blow hot and cold. Every day, you set aside time to make outbound calls and build momentum to achieve your sales goals. You know the direction of your career, you are honest with yourself about your strengths and weaknesses, and you invest your own time and money in your personal growth.

The successful Host is **Thoughtful**.

You constantly study and improve your Emotional Intelligence, so you can 'read' people and have a wide range of techniques to handle the situations that come up when dealing with customers. You are also thoughtful about your brand in the gaming industry and you go out of your way to protect your reputation for having Integrity.

In addition to all of these characteristics, the successful Host has **Passion**! Player Development is a lot of work, for sure, but based in so much passion.

> *"People say you need to have a lot of passion for what you're doing and it's totally true. The reason is because it's so hard that if you don't have it, any rational person would give up." Steve Jobs.*

Please consider sharing your passion and joining the Casino Player Development Association (C-PDA). The goal is to spread recognition of the value of Player Development and establish PD as a profession.

Final Thought

There is no question that our industry is undergoing changes and will continue to change in reaction to new technologies and new customer behavior. During the conversations for this book, some people even questioned the future of PD given that we live in a digital world. I believe PD will grow in importance because the human relationship will become the competitive advantage. Even online gaming companies are hiring PD professionals to establish 1:1 interaction with the very best players.

And I believe Player Development will grow in importance because of increased competition. Only a Host can truly secure the loyalty of highly valuable players. So, you are in a great position for a strong career. Keep reading, watching, and growing.

But now! Put the book down! Go get those customers! Hustle!

GLOSSARY

There are many different terms used across the Gaming industry for the same concept, so these are the terms we use in this Book.

Book of Business. This is a sales term, across different industries, for the list of people that you are trying to sell to. As a Casino Host, you have 300+ players coded to you, and that is your Book of Business. You are basically responsible for selling trips and amenities.

Churn. "Are you busy generating new customers but losing your existing customers at the same rate?" If a Host acquires 20 new players but allows 60 Active players to slip away because they are dissatisfied, then the Host is down by 40 valuable players.

Coded. A player that is coded to a Host in the Player Tracking System or a spreadsheet. There will typically be 300-400 players coded to each Host.

The **Comp Matrix** is a set of rules about who can get what kind of comp, and who can approve an override. For example, only a VP can approve a comp for alcohol in the steakhouse. For example, the value of a comp cannot exceed more than 10% of ADT for the last 30 days.

A **Comp Exception** means that someone has approved a comp that the guest did not qualify for, or that broke the rules of the Comp Matrix. The Finance/Audit team will be monitoring the comps to check for fraud or wastage, and you can expect to be asked about decisions that you made days and weeks ago. Hence it is always a good idea to make a note about your logic and who approved it.

Active. The Active players are making regular enough Trips with a high-end ADT. For example, 450+ ADT and 12+ trips over the last six months.

These players have visited 'recently' which has a different definition by Property and Market. If your casino serves local players within a two-hour drive, then 'recently' might be a trip within the last 3 months, but you may also have some high-end players that come in twice a year from a distant major city and deserve VIP attention.

In Database Marketing, we take a longer view so 'Active' tends to mean 'played in the last 12 months'. In Player Development, we are focused on a small set of highly valuable players who should be visiting with above average frequency, so 'Active' may mean 3 months.

Earned Benefit. In some Properties, it is considered a valuable benefit to be coded to a Host, and a player can 'earn' this VIP Service as part of their Tier benefits in the loyalty program. A player is automatically coded if their play is high enough and will be automatically de-coded if their play falls away.

Inactive. A player that used to play with a high ADT and frequency of trips but has not visited 'recently'. If the Player Development team can get these people back on property, then that is called **Reactivation**.

At Risk. A player 'at risk' is an Active player that is almost Inactive! For example, if your criteria for Active is that they have played with six months, then an Active player might be considered 'at risk' if they have not played for four months. You can focus the Player Development team on these at-risk players by setting a Retention Goal. For example, "80% of Active coded players must play at least once a Quarter."

Incliner and Decliner. We refer to a player as an Incliner if contribution is increasing because of increased trips, increased ADT, or both. Conversely, a player is Declining if they have few trips, lower ADT, or both.

New. A player that signed up within the last few days and has played with a high enough Theo to suggest they could be valuable in the future. These are sometimes referred to as **Dibbed** players meaning a Host has dibs on them, or as **Ghosted** to describe the fact that the Host is quietly monitoring the player.

Acquisition. A player that is not coded to a Host but is playing often enough, and with enough Theo, to be coded to a Host in the future. Many PD programs will monitor these players and assign a Host to reach out and develop them.

Valuable. Does a valuable player have a 200+ ADT or a 600+ ADT? The definition of valuable varies by Property and Market. A valuable player to a casino on the Strip is playing much higher than a valuable player in a casino in a rural area. But the 80:20 rule applies in both cases. Who are the 20% of players that are contributing 80% of revenue?

Profitable. If you want a lively discussion in your next team meeting, then initiate this debate about who is most profitable?

- Denise who plays 20 days each month with a 100 ADT and receives a free buffet?

- Or, Rob who plays twice a month with a 1000 ADT but demands the penthouse and a dinner comp, and drinks all the Jack Daniels in the VIP room?

Their total Theo per month is the same and Dee's expenses are less, so she is more profitable to the Casino. In most Properties, Rob will have a VIP Host because of his 500 ADT and Denise will not, with her 100 ADT. But some Properties use both ADT and total Theo as criteria for decisions in both Direct Mail and Player Development.

Upside Down. A player that is 'upside down' is consuming more expenses than is warranted by their Theo. Let's say the VP Marketing has set a maximum investment of 23% in players. A player is upside down if their total expenses for the month are $280 and their total Theo is $1000 i.e. investment is 28% of Theo.

Net Theo (Total Theo – Total Expenses) is sometimes used in the Host Goals to measure value. For example, the goal "Increase Net Theo from Active players by 10% over the same quarter last year" is measuring both an increase in Theo and a control on expenses

About the Author

Jackie has over 30 years in technology and business, and over 12 years in gaming. She loves Player Development professionals because you are all so nice!

Jackie co-founded the Casino Player Development Association and she publishes regular articles at playerdevelopment.com.

Her first degree is in Computer Science, her second degree is an MBA, and her introduction to gaming was via Caesars Entertainment. In 2009, Jackie co-founded Harvest Trends to provide affordable software solutions for casinos of all sizes and to level the playing field with 'the big guys'.

One solution is PowerHost; recognized by Casino Journal as an award-winning, innovative solution.

PowerHost is an affordable software solution for Hosts that lets you track your players, capture notes and preferences, and give each other Tasks. PowerHost has ratings from your Player Tracking System so it can automatically put your players into your Classifications and show your pace to Goals. And PowerHost can recommend who to call based on when the guest last played and when you last spoke to them. Learn more at www.harvesttrends.com.

Thank you for reading this book! Please send any feedback to me at jparker@harvesttrends.com.

27813687R00077

Made in the USA
Lexington, KY
05 January 2019